PRINCE ROLY

TONY ALEXANDER-WEBBER

Copyright © 2023 Tony Alexander-Webber

All rights reserved

The characters and events portrayed in this book are fictitious. Any similarity to real persons, living or dead, is coincidental and not intended by the author.

No part of this book may be reproduced, or stored in a retrieval system, or transmitted in any form or by any means, electronic, mechanical, photocopying, recording, or otherwise, without express written permission of the author.
Contact at smilepoetry@btinternet.com
All illustrations by author

*To Nicky, Jack, Miranda, and Doug.
Their love and support
my inspiration and motivation.*

*Also to our late beloved Queen Elizabeth II
who makes a guest appearance in our story.
I am sure she would have been amused.*

CONTENTS

Title Page
Copyright
Dedication
Chapter 1 Love In A Nutt-Shell   1
Chapter 2 Under The Duvet and The Weather   6
Chapter 3 Mum's The Word   12
Chapter 4 Here Today for the Heir Tomorrow   20
Chapter 5 The Water Baby   28
Chapter 6 Change the Baby   36
Chapter 7 What's in a Name ?   44
Chapter 8. The Christening Gets Carried Away   51
Chapter 9 Read All About It   59
Chapter 10 School, Surely Not   68
Chapter 11 A New Friend   74
Chapter 12 Double Figures   81
Chapter 13 The Adventure Begins   89

CHapter 14	Fellump, Fellump, Fellump!	95
Chapter 15	The Great Race	102
Chapter 16	The Olympic Challenge	111
Chapter 17	Royal Encounters	120
Chapter 18	The Heat Is On	128
Chapter 19	Finally The Final…Just!	134
Chapter 20	The Big Finish	143
Chapter 21	Sir Quiggly Comear's News	149
Chapter 22	Royal Visits	156
Chapter 23	What An Entrance	162
Chapter 24	Climb Every Mountain	167
Chapter 25	Look Over Your Shoulder	173
Chapter 26	A Steady Pair Of Hands	180

CHAPTER 1   LOVE IN A NUTT-SHELL

His Majesty King Richard Ricardo P. Nutt-Butter was the sole remaining descendant of the Nutt-Butter dynasty. The family had ruled the happy land of Artonia for hundreds of years. He was tall, elegant, slightly bonkers and ruled his kingdom kindly, with a certain wit and charm.

The nation was not rich, but was not poor. It made a good deal of steady cash from Artonian Blue Cheese. This was made from the milk of the highly distinguished Artonian Blue Cow. This particular breed of cow was fed on blue grass and bubble gum. This helped to make the cheese both light and bubbly and have a slightly spearmint tang to its taste. It sold well in exclusive restaurants throughout the world. Here well-heeled customers could indulge their taste buds with a little of this bubbly gumly cheese.

King Richard had a wonderful and also slightly dotty wife called Flotilla.

Flotilla had been on a walking tour of Artonia and had knocked on the palace door mistaking it for a rather grand hotel.

King Richard had happened to open the door.

"Good day to you." said King Richard with a beaming smile.

'Oh!" said Flotilla smiling back with an equally beaming smile. After quite a long pause Flotilla spoke.

"I have been walking for some hours and wondered if you served tea?"

"I would be delighted to serve you tea," said King Richard happily "and perhaps a slice of cake if you so wish?"

"That sounds, in a nut-shell, perfect. Thank you." replied Flotilla.

"Nutt-Shell!" exclaimed King Richard "Nutt-Butter. Any relation by chance?" he asked extending his right hand towards Flotilla.

"Not by chance, but perhaps by good fortune." replied Flotilla taking his right hand in hers and shaking it warmly.

King Richard led Flotilla into the palace. He soon made a pot of tea and gave her a slice of the coffee and walnut cake he had made earlier that day.

They talked with endless ease. Flotilla about her love of the life adventurous and Richard of his duties, joys and pride of being the King of Artonia. They got on like a house on fire. By the time their tea was over they had both fallen completely in love.

King Richard picked up his courage and spoke with a slight tremor in his voice.
"This has been such fun. Would it be possible that we could perhaps, that is to say... I was wondering if... I don't suppose you would consider... to be or not to be, that is the question...ummm...my, wife?"

Flotilla beamed again with a smile so bright it would have lit the darkest night and calmed the roughest sea. She then replied.
"I think that would be a marvellous idea. In answer to your question I am more than delighted to accept your proposal and to have you as my husband."
With that the royal love-birds became betrothed and the wedding date was set for 60 days henceforth and so forth. There were a great many royal proclamations and public announcements. These made the entire population of Artonia a good deal more than a little excited. Artonians, all three thousand, nine hundred and seventy four of them (last official census 1991) loved to have a party.

What better excuse was there than the marriage of their   beloved if slightly eccentric king.

During their countdown courtship the sweethearts found that they had lots in common other than both being slightly daft. Flotilla loved snooker and table tennis as well as   fishing. Those all happened to be amongst King Richard's favourite hobbies. Both of them enjoyed cooking and more importantly eating. They both had a great sense of fun, and a taste for doing things on the spur of the moment. Life would never be dull.

Their wedding was a spectacular event. The entire nation was treated to an A.F.C. Family Bucket with extra fries and a coleslaw side. The happy couple paraded through the city streets regaled in their finest robes.

The crowds cheered excitedly and the loyal subjects threw confetti and flower petals over the happy couple.

A band played joyously on their bendy instruments. They were the Royal Elastic Band after all. They offered a lively medley of popular tunes including Abba's greatest hits and   some grand funk soul brother stuff. This cut a groove with both the Royal VIP's and ordinary Artonian folk alike. There was dancing till Dawn came. Unfortunately Dawn was driving their minibus and she and the band had to go. The dancing sadly ceased. King Richard felt he should say a few words. The   crowds became hushed.

"Loyal subjects," began King Richard. "Today Flotilla has made me the happiest man in the kingdom. You my lovely people have blessed us by joining in our celebrations."

At this the crowd murmured contentedly and there was a polite round of applause. The King continued:

"This day has been touched by magic. By Royal Decree I declare that each year on this date there will be a national holiday. Then this joy and happiness can be remembered and our marriage celebrated."

A member of the crowd called out.

"Three cheers for His Majesty King Richard Ricardo P. Nutt-Butter and his beautiful if ever so slightly dotty wife Flotilla. Hip-Hip"

"Hooray!" bellowed the crowd with two more cheers and one for luck. The night then drew them all towards home and their duvets.

King Richard and his beloved Flotilla returned to the palace for a game of snooker and three sets of table tennis all of which the King lost. They then retired to the royal boudoir for a richly deserved and very happy and contented night's sleep.

CHAPTER 2 UNDER THE DUVET
AND THE WEATHER

Several blissful months later Queen Flotilla [for we must now use her full title] awoke one morning not feeling quite her normal self.

King Richard was busy in the kitchen making maple and blueberry flapjacks for himself and all of the royal household. With his love of cooking he often joined in with the kitchen staff preparing the daily fare which they all enjoyed at the palace. A royal maid whispered in his ear that the Queen was awake, but not feeling at her best. She had requested that His Majesty come up and see her at once.

King Richard flew up the stairs to the royal boudoir. He burst through the doors in a state of some anxiety.

"Flotilla, Flotsie, whatever's the matter my little cheesecake?" he asked.

"Oh Ricardillo please don't mention food. I'm afraid it makes me feel all funny in the tumsie-wumsie." the Queen replied.

"The tumsie wumsie, my little dumpling?" the King asked.

"Ricardillo, not dumplings either, please."

"Sorry… Suga..ah, ah, er… dearest one. Where does it hurt?" tried the King.

"It doesn't hurt my darling, it just doesn't feel quite right." said the Queen.

"Where doesn't it feel quite right my dearest? In the tumsie-wumsie?"

"Well yes, but all over really. Whatever can it be?" asked the Queen.

"Perhaps you are hungry Flotsie, some blueberry flapjacks with maple syrup will settle you down." suggested the King.

At the mention of the blueberry flapjacks, or perhaps it was the maple syrup, Flotilla pulled back the sheets and sprang from the bed.

She raced through to the royal bathroom with her hand firmly over her mouth. There were strange gurgling and rumbling sounds bubbling up from deep within. She slammed the door shut and left poor King Richard looking totally bemused and not a little guilty in the bedroom.

Several minutes later after some very unpleasant groans, rumbles and moans from within the bathroom there came the sound of running water. Flotilla finally returned to the bedroom, climbed back into bed and pulled the embossed golden duvet over her head. From within this enclave King Richard heard just a few words which included "food...twit..." and "...I warned him!"

"Dearest. Is there anything I can do?" asked the embarrassed King to his now definitely quite poorly wife "Anything at all?"

With mustered strength Flotilla gave her simple reply.
"Yes Richard...GO!"
With his head hung lower than an elephant's trunk King Richard slunk out of the bedroom. He felt very guilty for having made his beloved wife feel much worse. He was also very worried that Flotilla could be seriously ill.

His whirling mind worked hard to gather his thoughts. At last he summoned his much trusted Chief Advisor, Sir Quiggly Comear, to please join him in the royal library.

Sir Quiggly Comear was a wise old gentleman. He had as a young man passed three Artonian GCSE's. This was quite an achievement in a nation where Mastermind was dropped from the television schedules because no-one could think of any questions, let alone work out the answers. He knocked and entered the library in some trepidation. He could not remember such a commotion at the palace since the King's late father King Ringo Roscoe had stubbed his toe on a bowling ball. The King was always late, even before he had died. He was even late for his own funeral. The hearse driver had stopped at a lollipop shop to buy refreshments for the grave diggers.

"Your Majesty asked for me?" asked Sir Quiggly wriggling his ancient nose under his half moon glasses.

"Ah yes Quiggly. It's Her Majesty. She is not herself, not herself at all."

"Not herself Your Majesty?" puzzled Sir Quiggly "Then who might I ask is she?"

"No, no, no Quiggly. You don't follow my drift. Her Majesty is not quite feeling herself, not at all." said King Richard.

Sir Quiggly wondered what it might be that Her Majesty was feeling, but using all his intellectual powers decided that this might not be a good line of enquiry to pursue. A small door opened in the dusty back rooms of his brain and at last a tiny sesame seed sized idea flickered into life.

"Ah ha !" said Sir Quiggly.
"Ah ha?" replied the King.
"Ah ha Your Majesty. Could it be that Queen Flotilla

is in need of medical assistance."
" Why yes Quiggly, I do believe you could be right. That's it we do need medical assistance, and pretty pronto too."
"Certainly Your Majesty. I shall send for Dr.Erroneous Doodle the Surgeon Royal."

The King began to look anxious.
"You do suppose she will be all right Quiggly? I should be most distressed if anything were to happen to the Queen."
Sir Quiggly gave his warmest smile and re-assured King Richard.

"Oh, I am certain it is nothing serious Your Majesty. Probably just a bit of indigestion or something of that sort."
"Quite, quite. Then why are we calling for the Surgeon Royal? Surely that sounds far more serious?"
"We are sending for the Surgeon Royal Your Majesty   because it is better to be safe than to be sorry," Sir Quiggly cleared his throat " and, because Erroneous is the only medically trained man in the Kingdom!"

The King replied.
"Very well Sir Quiggly, I shall let you proceed. Her Majesty was in quite some distress when I left her a few minutes ago. And she was not best pleased with

my efforts to help. Something needs to be done!"

"And done it will be your highness. I shall send my young secretary Scudamore as quickly as possible to fetch the good Doctor." said Sir Quiggly, bowing as he left the Royal Library.

Scudamore was swiftly despatched post haste to fetch the Surgeon Royal Doctor Erroneous Doodle. His surgery was located some distance from the palace on the far side of the city.

CHAPTER 3   MUM'S THE WORD

Doctor Erroneous Doodle had been to medical school in London, England and had really tried hard to keep up with his studies. Unfortunately the goodly man had also fallen in love with the great city's double decker red buses. He had spent every free hour travelling the capital's never ending streets on any number of these beautiful vehicles. He learned every route, every turn and every traffic light. Eventually, even if blindfolded, he could sit on any bus at any time and know exactly where he was within the great City of London.

Sadly when it came to his final year examinations to qualify as a doctor the two subjects became merged into one within his bright but flitty mind.

He confused cardiac arrest with Camden Lock, water on the knee with Waterloo Bridge, pneumonia with New Bond Street and disorders of the pancreas with St Pancras Station. He couldn't tell his Piccadilly from his pelvis or his fibula from his Fulham Park Road.
The examiners were puzzled for he had always seemed so bright in class. His answers had a ring of correctness about them even if they were a little bizarre. For example to the question "Where would one find the main colon?" he had written; "Catch the number 4 to Aldwych. Follow the intestinal Strand until you get to Nelson's Colon in Trafalgar Square."

The examiners noted that there was lots of very sound medical information in his answers. They also noted that Erroneous was the first and only ever student from the obscure country of Artonia. They decided therefore that it would probably be safe enough to grant him the title of Doctor of Medicine. Thus he became Doctor Erroneous Doodle M.D. with a C.L.O.T. (Certificate in London's Organised Transport) thrown in for good measure.

On this particular morning the good doctor was munching marmite soldiers and reading his latest Red Route-Master Annual. Erroneous heard a prolonged and pronounced banging on his front door. Reluctantly he put the book down, picked up his stethoscope and went to attend to his visitor. He thought it must be a patient in need of some care. There stood the rather breathless, red faced and panting Scudamore who tried to speak.

"Doc...tor...I ..."
"Now, now dear chap, let's get you into the surgery no need for words eh!"
"But, her, her, her high, her high..." gasped Scudamore.
"High temperature? Yes, yes I can see that. Now do come and sit down while I examine you properly."
At this Erroneous led the young Scudamore quite forcibly into his surgery and sat him in his patient's chair. He put a wooden spatula in his mouth, pressed down very hard on the tongue and said:
"Could you say aah please?"
"Aaaaaaaah !" squealed Scudamore in some pain.
"Oooh dear I don't like the sound of that. Any other symptoms?" asked Erroneous. He removed the spatula from some distance down the poor young man's throat.
Scudamore took this opportunity to remove himself from the chair and gain a few paces between himself and the over enthusiastic doctor.
"Doctor please. There has been a mistake."
"Mistake? But I haven't made my diagnosis yet." replied Erroneous.
Scudamore continued bravely.
"No, no can we please start again. I am Scudamore

and I am a palace aid."

"Right, and I am Doodle and I like lemonade."

"I have come from the palace for the King." he said.

"But he's not here, at least I don't think so. Is he?"

Scudamore was getting exasperated, but he remembering the urgency of his mission he ploughed ahead regardless.

"No Doctor Doodle. His Majesty is not here, he is back at the palace. He is very worried about his wife Her Majesty The Queen who seems to have become unwell."

"Unwell? Poor Her Majesty. What's wrong with her?" he asked.

"But that is why I have come to see you Doctor." said Scudamore.

"Oh, so are you unwell as well?" asked Erroneous.

Scudamore at this moment considered taking himself off to be trained in medicine. He thought that the seven year course might perhaps provide a swifter conclusion to the current crisis. However he maintained his focus and standing in a tall and controlled way continued.

"Doctor Doodle!"

"Mister Scoodle?"

"Please get your doctor's bag and come with me straight away to the palace."

"I'll do that then."

"We must not dawdle Doodle"

"I will not dawdle Scoodle"

"Goodle, I mean good! Now please Doctor let's be

gone."
And with that last little exchange of nonsense the two hurried swiftly across the busy city's streets back to the palace.

King Richard was waiting for them anxiously by the royal front door. Too worried to speak the King mumbled a few coughs and splutters. He led the Surgeon Royal to the royal boudoir to attend upon Queen Flotilla. The door was closed by the good doctor and the King was left to pace nervously up and down the upstairs corridor. He then went down the stairs, back up once more, back along the corridor and back down the stairs again. This continued for several minutes although to King Richard it felt like hours. Finally after a good deal of wear and tear of the royal carpets the bedroom door re-opened and the doctor reappeared.
The King spoke first.
"Well Doctor?"
"Yes thank you Your Majesty. Good of you to ask."
"No, no, the Queen?."
"Ah yes of course, Her Majesty."
"Well?"
"I should say so. Never been better."
"Never better!" spluttered King Richard
"Quite so Your Majesty. All done and dusted. Now move down the bus please I have to be back in Hackney Wick for the number 6 connection by midday."

The King asked again.

"But what is wrong with Her Majesty? Please say good doctor, as I really am beside myself."

This puzzled the doctor who looked to the left and to the right of the King. He could see nothing so scratched his head in puzzlement and said,

"Can't see it myself. Anyway Your Majesty, go and see your good wife and she will explain all. Must dash. Sworn to secrecy. Mum's the word!"

At that the doctor skipped down the stairs shouting.

"Ding-ding, hold very tight please. Move down the bus!"

He then disappeared out through the front door. The King meanwhile braced himself, knocked and went into their bedroom to see Flotilla. She was sat up in bed quite transformed. No longer mal-de-mer but simply magnificent and smiling a momentous smile from ear to glorious ear.

"Flotilla?"

"Ricardillo!"

"Dearest Flotilla are you cured?"

"Darling husband, you make me sound like a piece of bacon."

"Bacon?" queried the King "so you are all right with food again my dearest dumpling?"

"All right...ALL RIGHT!" called Flotilla in less than royal like tones, "I am more than all right, I am blooming starving. I would like pancakes, chocolate chip ice cream, crisps and a pork pie for starters. Perhaps for lunch we could have some jellied eels with raspberries."

King Richard looked puzzled.

"Rather a strange combination my sweet, would you not just prefer a slice of toast?"

The Queen's smile was growing wider and wider. She could no longer keep herself calm.

"Toast will simply not do Ricardillo, not at all."

"Not do at all?" asked His Majesty

"No, it will not do at all. Not now that I am eating for two!"

"For two?" repeated the King glancing about the room quite dreamily as if expecting to see a guest or visitor.

"For two!" repeated Flotilla.

There was then a few seconds of silence that felt like an eternity. A cog turned slowly in His Majesty's brain. At last, very slowly, but with the gathering speed of a winter sunrise, his face began to give a clue that at last the proverbial penny was finally dropping.

"For two Flotilla? You are…you are…"

The Queen stepped in just in case the child was to be born before its future arrival was discussed.

"I am my dearest darling, I am…I am going to have …"

The King interrupted, " A baby!"

"A baby my sweetness. An heir to the throne, and you will become a father."

At that King Richard Ricardo P Nutt-Butter took

a step forward, raised his fluttering eyes to the heavens, drew an enormous breath and promptly fainted. He fell as flat as an ironing board on to the royal rug next to the bed. He was out cold.

Queen Flotilla stepped from the bed and patted her royal husband's head.

"I presume that means you are pleased my darling." With that she picked up the bedside phone and spoke with Sir Quiggly Comear. She updated him of her most excellent news and then asked if Scudamore might once again venture across to Doctor Doodle's.

It appeared that the King had taken a funny turn.

CHAPTER 4   HERE TODAY FOR THE HEIR TOMORROW

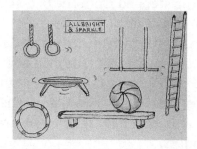

The birth of any baby is a joyous and wonderful thing. The birth of a Royal Artonian baby is an event that grips the imagination and excitement of the whole nation tighter than a sweet toothed limpet on a lollipop.

Soon there were dozens of busy hands with even busier knitting needles click clacking away at furious speed. They were engaged in the production of a vast array of brightly coloured bootees, romper suits, cardigans and hats for the eagerly expected heir. Blue for a boy and pink for a girl had never been a tradition in Artonia. It had always been a dazzlingly rainbow nation full of all colours and more than a little sparkle. Every colour you imagine was being knitted and sown into a delightful royal   wardrobe for the future prince or princess.

Back in the palace now some months on His Majesty King Richard and Her Majesty Queen Flotilla were eating breakfast and talking babies. Thank goodness, the right way round. Flotilla's diet had returned to a more normal regime apart from the occasional midnight munch of waffles with garlic sausage and piccalilli.

That actually does sound quite yummy.

The royal arrival was being discussed in quite excited tones. If the happy couple ever had any disagreements they were always resolved quickly and never with any unpleasantness. Their rallies were a bit like the tennis matches at Wimbledon. Points won and lost on the bounce of the ball, before the conversation and the game moved on.

King Richard serves. "The child will need a nanny of course."

"Why of course?" returns Queen Flotilla before King Richard volleys back.

"Well I had a Nanny dearest and look at me."

Flotilla scoops the ball in the air and sets up a dangerous lob.

"But I didn't have a Nanny dearest, and look at me!"

King Richard watches this one carefully and thinks about running back but decides it is beyond him. Too risky a shot to be attempted. The ball bounces perfectly on the line and the point is won by Queen Flotilla. Fifteen love.

Her Majesty serves this time, throwing the ball high in the air just before striking it perfectly.

"We shall bring our baby up Ricardillo, because you and I are beautiful people so our baby will be beautiful too, agreed?" An ace, thirty love.

The King tries another serve.

"But with all our royal duties my sweet might we not need a little assistance from time to time. Another pair of hands so to speak?"

Flotilla sees this one coming and is straight up to the net to send it back at some pace.

"If you are making a speech I can hold the baby. If I am opening a fete you can hold the baby. What then is the problem?"

Forty love.

The Queen serves once more, this time for the game. "I love you so much Ricardillo and I want us to bring up this baby together. We should care and share duties like those musketeer chaps, all for one and one for all. What do you say my darling?"

The ball bounces beyond his reach and King Richard rushes to the net.

"Game set and match my dearest darling. Come and give me a hug."

Queen Flotilla runs round the table to give her happy husband a huge hug. This is getting quite tricky now as the baby bump is already at quite a size. More volley ball than beach ball but something that needed navigation all the same.

After a few cuddly moments the royal pair return to their breakfast. There is once more the sound of toast being cheerfully chomped and eggs being daintily dipped and slurped. A knock on the door interrupts the feasting. Sir Quiggly Comear enters with a dutiful bow to both Their Majesties who finish their mouthfuls and politely nod back.

"Ah Sir Quiggly, a good day to you dear fellow, good day. To what do we owe the pleasure, what news dear boy what news?"

"Your Majesties, it is time for your ten o'clock appointment" said Sir Quiggly in a matter of fact tone.

"Ten o'clock already, and we have an appointment. How very grand, how very grand indeed. With whom is this appointment? I can hardly wait."

Queen Flotilla sighed, "Oh Richard you really are a scatter wallop. You agreed we could meet today with the royal designers to decide upon the decoration of the new nursery."

"Royal designers?" asked the King.

"Yes dearest. Allbright and Sparkle. They are here by Royal Appointment.

"Another appointment, dear me, will we fit it all in?"

"No, no, you made the royal appointment some years ago dearest."

"And they've only showed up today! Well they're jolly late and that's jolly rude."

Sir Quiggly tries to get things back on track.

"Your Majesty if I might explain, Messrs' Allbright and Sparkle, whom you appointed as your royal designers some years ago, are here for their ten o'clock appointment. They are here now and they are without."

"Without what?" queried the King only just beginning to touch base.

"Without the door, in the corridor Your Majesty."

The King looked puzzled once more. "Were they supposed to bring one then?"

"Bring what Your Majesty?" replied Sir Quiggly himself now also losing the plot.

"The door of course. You said they were without."

Queen Flotilla rose to her full height and with due authority commanded her husband to stop twittering. She asked Sir Quiggly to send the two renowned designers into the royal dining room straight away.

King Richard brushed the crumbs off his waistcoat and tried to look royally important whilst Flotilla stepped forward to meet the two gentlemen. They swept into the room with a flourish of extravagant bowing. The flamboyance of their entrance was only matched by their orange and avocado dungarees, cherry red boots and strawberry check shirts. The King thought for a moment that chef had sent up some sort of exotic fruit salad.

He slowly remembered that the appointment was with designers. A certain artistic licence in their dress was to be expected.

The Queen got things moving.
"Now gentlemen you are aware that we are

expecting a very happy addition to the royal household in a few months." Messrs Allbright and Sparkle clapped their hands in unison and beamed warmly at the Queen.

"The King and I would like you to design and create a nursery for our future child. We want it be somewhere that will be exciting and stimulating."

The pair looked at each other, nodded and then turned back. The King added his two pennies worth.

"It must not be a dull room. We want an exciting place for an exciting baby. Somewhere with a bit of buzz and a lot of bounce!"

"Buzz?" pondered Sparkle to himself.

"Bounce?" wondered Allbright deep in thought.

"Yes. His Majesty is exactly right, buzz and bounce; bounce and buzz. Any ideas gentlemen, top of your heads and so forth?" asked Flotilla.

The two creative thinkers gazed into each other's eyes. You could almost sense some little sparks jumping across between them. Suddenly Sparkle stepped over to the dining table and climbed on top. Having grabbed three oranges from the fruit bowl he began to juggle.

Allbright not to be outdone went into a forward roll then stood up upon his hands and started walking across the floor. Sparkle leapt from the table and grabbing the lowest arm of the chandelier began to swing across the room gathering speed as he did so. He hooked his legs over the chandelier and allowed his body to flop upside down. Now his hands were facing towards the floor.

Allbright stood up, leapt up to catch his partner's arms and was carried in a great sweep across the room and back. After three or four swoops he let go his grip to perform a summersault landing at the feet of the royal couple. Both the King and Queen were whooping with excitement at the spectacle. Sparkle swung down from the chandelier and joined his partner.

The Queen clapped her hands in delight as the King joined in with one or two calls of bravo, bravo.

"Gentlemen, gentlemen brilliance, pure brilliance. A circus for our child. What a wonderful idea." said Flotilla.

"And for us my dearest, and for us. Can't have the little chap or chapess being lonely eh?" added the King.

With no words being spoken it was agreed the design for the nursery would be a circus. A beautiful room full of swings and hoops .Things to bounce on and things to bounce off. A space to feed the imagination and thrill the heart. The two gentlemen quickly sketched some designs which of course met with royal approval.

The two colourful designers Allbright and Sparkle both bowed and flourished their way out of the royal dining room. Their mission accomplished and their work ready to start.

The Queen sat down to read her latest selection from the library "How To Have An Amazing Baby", whilst the King tried rather unsuccessfully to juggle with just one orange.

CHAPTER 5   THE WATER BABY

The birth of the royal baby was just a week or so away. King Richard Ricardo P Nutt-Butter the expectant father was beside himself with anticipation and excitement. Like a bottle of ginger beer strapped to the back of a pizza delivery bike, he really was all shook up and ready to pop.

Every few minutes or so it seemed he was fussing over Flotilla with an "Any news dearest?" or some such comment. This was driving Her Majesty almost mad. If she coughed, sneezed or simply sighed the King was ready to send Scudamore or one of the other palace staff, hot foot across the city to fetch the Surgeon Royal. At each such occurrence Queen Flotilla would have to forestall or cancel the instruction and then calm His Majesty down. You would have thought it was the King who was about to give birth. In many ways Flotilla thought that this was not such a bad idea. But 'ho-and-hum', nature would take its natural course as every woman understood.

King Richard was practicing a trick at the snooker table trying to pot three balls in one shot. He had done this by accident a few weeks earlier when trailing Her Majesty by some 42 points. He did not go on to win the game despite Flotilla giving him an extra twenty points for being such a "clever boy". It was the closest he had ever come to beating her since they had been married.

Flotilla came quietly into the games room to speak with her husband.

"Ricardillo darling, it's about the baby."

King Richard miscued his shot causing the white ball to leave the table and fly through the air straight towards the Queen's head. Flotilla flicked out her left hand quite casually as if swatting a fly. She caught the ball and returned it to the table in one fluid motion.

"The b...b...b...baby. It's about to happen. Lie down put your feet up. I'll call for the doctor. No I won't I'll go myself. No I won't leave you on your own, I'll...I'll... I'll..."

"You will calm down Richard. I am not having the baby."

"Well you have put on a bit of weight then!"

"No you ninny! I am not having the baby today. I just want to talk about it, that's all."

"Aah, I see." gasped the King his heartbeat slowly edging down from about the 200 mark to more normal levels. "You want to talk about it Flotsie, no problem, fire ahead."

Queen Flotilla picked up her favourite cue, moved the white ball to the "D" and proceeded to pot the three carefully positioned balls in one shot. "I say!" frumped His Majesty. The Queen put down the cue and continued.

"I want to have the baby underwater."

King Richard slapped his hand down on the snooker table and laughed.

"Ha ha, for one moment then my darling I thought I could have sworn you said you wanted to have the baby underwater. I am sorry. What was it you did say?"

"What you just said." Answered the Queen.

"What I just said?"

"Yes Richard what you just said. Underwater."

"Was it my idea then?" asked the King.

"No dear it was mine, or at least I read about it in a magazine. 'Beautiful Births For Beautiful Babies.' It is the latest thing and all perfectly safe." explained the Queen.

The King continued, somewhat concerned.

"It doesn't sound very safe to me, being born underwater. What if the baby cannot swim! I had to have loads of lessons before I could swim." he said.

Flotilla explained, "The baby won't need lessons darling, when baby is born it will pop up to the top like a buoy."

"But what if it's a girl?" he asked.

"It doesn't matter, it will still pop up like a buoy."

The King sat down. "Now I am totally confused. Boys will be boys but girls will be boys too. It sounds so complicated Flotsie."

Flotilla continued with her reassurance and explanation.

" It isn't Richard, not at all. I have ordered a special birthing pool. Doctor Erroneous is happy, I am happy and all you have to do is be there."

"Why yes of course I'll be there, to hold your hand my darling."

Flotilla clarified once again.

"No Richard you'll be in the pool with me."

"In the pool?" asked the King.

"Yes."

"With you?"

"Yes."

"Swimming?"

"No Richard not swimming! Helping! You will be helping our baby to be born." she explained.

"Oh goodness. Me, an underwater midwife. How wonderful will that be." smiled the King

Flotilla laughed gently and gave her happy husband a big royal hug.

The very next day the birthing pool arrived and was set up in the circus nursery. It fitted in beautifully with the other oddities in the room and looked perfectly at home. It was filled with fresh water with His Majesty overseeing the entire process. He made certain that all the temperature controls and cleaning filters were working correctly. He did not want himself, his wife and their new baby to be either cooked or frozen. They were neither lobsters nor penguins.

The pool was royal size and therefore some 12 foot in diameter. King Richard thought that distance was about enough for a proper swim. But he knew that he was not allowed in the water until baby-day. This, as it turned out, was just three days later.

It was at 3 o'clock in the morning and His Majesty was in the middle of a delightful dream. He was just about to be presented with the World Snooker Championship Trophy. He had just won the final, 18 frames to zero, before an adoring and jubilant crowd. As he stretched out his arms to receive the trophy he felt a sharp pain in his ribs as the Queen dug her elbow into his side. Snapped from his reverie he heard her speak to him in calmer tones than her jab would have suggested.

"Richard, it is time."

"Time for breakfast dearest?"

"No Richard not breakfast, baby."

"Oh jolly good, night-night then darling."

The Queen waited! As sure as thunder follows lightning after about five silent seconds King Richard erupted.

"BABY! Man the pumps! Good gracious me!

Now, don't panic dearest remember to breathe, remember to breathe. Breathe in, Hooooo, breathe out, Haaaaaa, in Hooooo, out Haaaaaa."

"Richard!" said the Queen firmly.

"Yes?"

"Do just shush and listen."

"Yes dear."

Queen Flotilla gave some calm instructions to her very excited husband. Awaken Sir Quiggly. Arrange for the Surgeon Royal to be collected (really this time). Prepare the birthing pool and, perhaps he could have a nice cup of tea sent up. That would be wonderful.

His Majesty's brain went into overtime and remarkably he carried out all of these tasks in a very sensible manner, correctly and in the right order!

Flotilla put on her special birthing gown. Hearing that Doctor Erroneous Doodle had arrived, she made her way through to the birthing pool in the nursery.

As she entered the gently lit room she was met by the sight of what she thought at first was a giant green frog. It was of course King Richard. He was wearing a bright green wet suit complete with flippers, mask and snorkel. In his left hand was a small fishing net.

"Richard what are you doing?" asked the Queen.

The King saluted with his right hand and called across the room.

"All present, and ready for action. Sub-Aqua

Midwife Nutt-Butter reporting for duty my love."
Flotillas body was already telling her that there really might not be enough time for an extended discussion. She gave up any possible chance of arguing with her beloved and climbed very carefully into the warm and relaxing water. King Richard, appropriately for his attire, leap-frogged over the side to join his wife in the pool. This created a tidal wave that surged across the room just as the good doctor arrived in the nursery to oversee proceedings.

"I say!" said Erroneous "What awful weather to be out driving a bus. Have you all got your tickets?"

Flotilla sighed and resigned herself to fate and to focus on the imminent arrival of the much awaited baby.

There followed some three hours and a considerable amount of effort from Her Majesty. With one final push the baby was born into the steady and safe hands of King Richard. He lifted the delightful special delivery carefully up out of the water and into the waiting arms of Queen Flotilla.

The King spoke.

"Well done my darling, well done...Mummy! And you were right it is a boy."

"And well done you too my darling, you were marvellous Ricardillo...Daddy!"

Both were just about to burst into howling sobs of joy when their son and heir opened his lungs. He

took in a great gulp of air then emitted his first enormous cry.
He beat them both to it, turning their tears into laughter.

The Doctor beamed contentedly and assured that all was more than well withdrew from the nursery. He set off to spread the good news leaving the now three members of the royal family to get to know one another on their own.

CHAPTER 6   CHANGE THE BABY

It was just a few days after the birth of their wonderful baby. Neither Her Majesty Queen Flotilla nor her devoted husband King Richard had been able to get much if any sleep. His Majesty in particular was finding it hard to function at more than about ten per cent of his normal brain power. This as we have already gathered was not anything to get too excited about in the first place. The expression "the lights are on but nobody's in" was cruel but accurate. His tiredness meant that in effect, a few of the royal brain cells had temporarily 'fallen down the back of the sofa' and would need retrieving after some serious sleep.

The Queen, having fed the royal baby, was sat in a comfy armchair in a cosy corner of the circus nursery quietly nodding. King Richard was in the kitchen preparing his wife some toasted muffins with peach jam.   He hoped they would revive her flagging spirits. He placed the scrummy platter, together with a mug of hot chocolate on a tray and wobbled wearily back up the palace stairs to the nursery.

On entering the room all was quiet. The baby was flat on his back and sound asleep. His arms and legs were spread wide. It made him look like a brightly coloured starfish. Occasional happy gurgles bubbled up from his contented lips. His full tummy helped him to slumber.

The King tiptoed across the room and placed the tray carefully on the small table next to Her Majesty's armchair. He gently tried to wake his wife, laying a hand upon her right shoulder and speaking softly.

"Oh sweetheart." No response.

"Oh mummykins." Still no response. A gentle push to the royal shoulder.

"Your Majesty! Snackeroo time!" Nothing.

King Richard placed a hand upon each of Her Majesty's shoulders and with increasing vigour started rocking her back and forth.

"Flotilla, wak-ey wak-ey, it's mu-ffin time." His voice grew steadily louder and matched the rhythm of his rocking."

"and…plum…jam…and…a…mug…of…hot…choc…o…late!"

Flotilla's head was flapping backwards and

forwards like a slightly bemused woodpecker warming up on an ancient oak tree. The motion had thrown her mouth open and with each rock she was making an unusual sound.

A little like a motorbike revving up.

Varrrummm...varrrummm...varrummmm."

After some several seconds King Richard turned the engine off. This allowed Flotilla's head to flop back against a cushion. With a few "nyum, nyum, nyums" the extremely tired new mum drifted back off into a deep and much needed sleep.

"Oh bother!" said the King. He then proceeded to eat all the muffins and down the hot chocolate in one long creamy gulp.

"Waste not, what not and so on" he muttered before remembering that he too was very, very tired and would also like to have a little bobos. He curled up on the tiger shaped sofa resting his royal head on a fluffy pillow. With his thumb firmly in his mouth and his bottom in the air he fell instantly to sleep.

However, at that very moment the infant Prince, [as yet unnamed due to Their Majesties inability to agree on names] decided to wake up. This was partly due to the aroma of the hot chocolate. His senses had picked up on this as something good to look forward to in the future.

The main cause of his waking up was his nappy being decidedly damp. Like all babies his instincts knew that something should happen to sort that out. Without any words to come to his aid his young Majesty did what all babies do. He filled his lungs, opened his mouth and began to cry.

Every baby has different cries for different requests. These grow more elaborate as the baby gets older. One will mean "feed me", another "cuddle me", and yet another "entertain me with gooby-goo noises and funny faces". This one meant "I am wet, I don't like being wet. Sort me out!"
Unfortunately it was His and not Her Majesty who woke up straight away.

"Hang on Bertie, I'll fetch the gerbil...eh, what? Oh it's babykins. What's up young fella?"
The Queen was half awake from the infant's cries. In her part dreamy semi-awake state she muttered, " Change the baby Ricardillo. It's time to change the baby." After which, with all reserves used up she fell back into a deep, deep sleep.

Now in the first few days of the baby's life King Richard had been a perfect father in every way except that he had not yet been fully involved with the "Nappy Department". That, together with his own confused and exhausted state did not mean a swift and easy solution to the baby's current problem.
"Change? Change the baby? First I've heard of it," said the King talking to himself. "Still, Flotsie

knows best. Come on then little chap time to change you. Off we go."

King Richard pattered across the nursery and with two strong hands whisked the crying baby from his cot. The young Prince now safely in his father's arms quietened quickly down. He did not realise what potential peril he was in.

The King left the Queen asleep in the nursery and walked a little unsteadily down the stairs. All was calm.

"Right," thought the King "Now where do I go to change a baby?"

At this moment Sir Quiggly's secretary Scudamore happened to walk across the main hallway. Here he found the King standing, swaying with tiredness, and looking both lost and puzzled.

"Might I be of assistance Your Majesty?" asked Scudamore in his usual polite manner.

"Ah, Scudamore yes you might. Her Majesty has asked me to go and change the baby, and I am not sure where one goes to do that."

"Well Your Majesty, I would hazard a guess that the nursery is the best place for that sort of operation."

"The nursery? But I have just come from there and I didn't see any."

"See any what Your Majesty?" asked Scudamore a little puzzled himself.

"Any other babies. If I am to change this one, I will need a suitable replacement. Otherwise the Queen will be most upset."

Scudamore suddenly saw the gravity of the situation. He could see that His Majesty was very, very tired. There were indeed bags under the King's eyes the size of suitcases. In this dream like state the King had obviously got the idea that changing the baby meant exchanging it for another. And the King appeared quite determined to complete his mission despite his exhausted state.

Scudamore thought quickly and then spoke.

"Your Majesty was right to ask me. I can sort that out for you as quick as a flash, I know just the place."

"You do? Oh wonderful, shall we be off then?"

"No, no Your Majesty, I would not dream of getting you to venture out, it is a horrid evening. If you'll hand me the little chap I'll get it sorted whilst perhaps you could go and have a short nap."

"A nap? I say that does sound wonderful. I don't think I've had a nap for days." yawned the King.

"So if you would just pop the Prince over to me sir?"

"To you?" asked the King

"To me."

"To you?" repeated the King

"Yes Your Majesty, to me…please."

"Are you sure?"

"Absolutely." said a determined Scudamore

And then with just a moment's more hesitation the King passed the baby carefully over into the safe and greatly relieved hands of Scudamore.

"I say," said the King," My arms are very damp. I didn't think the little chap would be so heavy as to make me sweat that much."

With that the King turned round. Rather like a pinball zigzagged his way unsteadily up the stairs bouncing wearily from bannister to bannister. When he reached the landing he slipped silently back into the nursery. He collapsed once more on the tiger sofa and fell soundly asleep.

Downstairs Scudamore looked at the little Prince and sighed.

"Okay Young Majesty, let's go and get some help to have you sorted. I think your Ma and Pa need to get a good night's sleep. It will be good for them and I think quite good for you too!"

Scudamore held the baby very carefully at arm's length due to his very soggy state. He carried him towards the staff quarters. There he found the Royal Housekeeper Doris Morris who he knew had a young family herself. She might be able to help him.

"Help!" said Scudamore holding his precious bundle.

"Oh dear!" said Doris "Do we have a wee problem?"

"I'm afraid so Doris, very much a 'wee' problem." said Scudamore

"Hand the 'wee' fella over then, but don't go away. Another pair of hands is very useful!"

Between the two of them the young Prince was washed, newly nappied and changed into dry clothes. As quietly as mice in cotton wool slippers they tiptoed back into the nursery and popped him back into his cot. With just a couple of contented gurgles the Prince too fell soundly and deeply asleep.

Scudamore and Doris Morris crept out of the nursery leaving the entire royal family in a blissful state of sleep. They stayed that way until the first light of the next gloriously sunny day.

CHAPTER 7   WHAT'S IN A NAME ?

The Queen was the first to wake up. She saw that it was now daylight and that meant a whole night had passed with no baby interruptions. Slightly anxious she looked across the nursery and smiled to see both of her 'boys'. Sound asleep with thumbs in mouths and bottoms up. Like father like son.

"It must be the Nutt-Butter 'butt' position" thought Flotilla who smiled warmly to herself. She felt tickety-boo after a full night's sleep. As she began to stir so did King Richard and the baby.

"Aaah, Ricardillo, well done, you changed the baby without any problems."

At the word 'changed' His Majesty snapped fully awake. His hazy memory of the previous evening blurred into a confusion between dream and reality. He sprang from the sofa and quickly went to the cot. He happily confirmed to himself that the baby was the same little chap that had been there for the past few days. Relieved, he plucked him from his nest and gave him a good morning hug. He then handed him over to the Queen for his breakfast.

"I am awfully hungry my darling. Did you not mention muffins and hot chocolate or something?"said the Queen.

King Richard tapped last night's empty tray gently under the sofa out of view.

"Yes my dearest, you are absolutely right. I shall go and prepare them."

"Thank you Richard, and perhaps some bacon and eggs would be delicious too."

"Of course my sweet."

"And maybe a banana, I do seem to be a tad peckish."

"Right-oh! Back in ten dearest!" and having said that he picked up the old tray discretely and left the nursery.

At the bottom of the stairs Scudamore was sorting through the morning post. This still consisted mainly of cards congratulating the King and Queen on the birth of their baby boy. As His Majesty passed by Scudamore stopped and spoke.

"Good morning Your Majesty, a pleasant sleep I hope?"

"Yes thank you Scudamore." His Majesty paused as a feint memory stirred.

"I beg pardon Scudamore but did we meet late last evening by any chance?"

"Only briefly Your Majesty, you were wishing to change the young Prince so I simply offered to help. Your Majesty was quite obviously extremely tired."

"Indeed, yes I think I was. I also have this strange feeling Scudamore that I may have been going to do something that might have been a little bit silly."

'A little bit!' thought Scudamore to himself 'as dangerously daft as possible I would have thought.'

Then out loud he replied

"Not at all Your Majesty, all was well."

Scudamore smiled at the King who smiled back with a vague sense of understanding passing between them. King Richard nodded.

Scudamore nodded back very politely.

They both continued with their mornings.

Back in the nursery some while later Queen Flotilla was wide awake. Fully refreshed she wanted to talk. King Richard was gently trying to wind the baby. He was rubbing the baby's back warmly up and down with the child sprawled gently across the royal knees.

"Richard we cannot keep calling the baby Baby. Baby must have a proper name."

"Of course my dearest. Any two names beginning with R, that's the tradition."

"Oh really Richard!" complained the Queen.

"That would do I suppose, but I'm already Richard and Really really isn't a proper name." laughed the King.

"Now you are being ridiculous Richard, and before you say otherwise I am not suggesting Ridiculous Richard as a name. So please do not say that I do!"

"But I did say I do, when we were married dearest, and so did you. Therefore, as we both did an 'I do' we are the King and Queen of Artonia. As such we must maintain some traditions. The first born must always have two names beginning with R. We have had dear Roberto Rodriguez, Rosie Rosetta, Raoul Romerez, Raquel Rihanna, RufusRossetti and of course dearest papa, Ringo Roscoe to name but a few.".

"I know Richard, I know, I just wondered if we might change the tradition."

At the word change, His Majesty shuddered.

He continued.

"Dearest Flotsie, this is the one thing I must insist on. You know that in all other matters I always agree to your wonderful ideas."

This was indeed the case. His Majesty very rarely had any original ideas, and was more than happy that Flotilla held his hand and led the way. The Queen conceded.

"Very well my darling. The two R's it will be and I suppose the P. must remain?"

"What would a Nutt-Butter be without a P.?" replied the King with a quizzical look.

"Quite." replied the Queen who then began to try and think of some agreeable names that began with R. She thought of Raymond, Ralph, Rizzo,

Randolph, Rudyard, Ryan, Renaldo, Rory and then Rex.

"Ooh," said Flotilla "I quite like Rex."

"But Rex means King. You cannot call our son and heir Rex. That would mean 'King King'. No, no that will not do. And might I add that it does sound a bit dog-like dear." said the King.

"Dog like!" exclaimed Flotilla.

"Yes, you know. Here Rex, good boy, go fetch."

"Well we could call him Rover and be done with it."

"Now, now Flotsie don't give up." calmed His Majesty.

"Do you not have any relatives with a name beginning with an R my darling?"

"Well yes. There was a great uncle called Reginald, but he was a bit dotty so they say."

"Perfect," replied the King, "But we won't say dotty my dearest, just 'full of character'. Now what goes well with Reginald? What would balance that out? We could have Romeo, Roger, Romulus or what about the name Roland?"

The Queen pondered for a minute.

"Prince Roland Reginald! That does have a certain ring to it. We could call him Roly. What do you say Ricardillo?"

"Oh yes, I like it, Prince Roly really does rock! Well done Flotsie. Of course one day he'll have the whole name and title. King Roland Reginald P. Nutt-Butter. Suitably splendid. Are we in agreement my dearest?"

"Yes, I think that indeed we are Ricardillo." said the Queen.

So saying the happy couple sealed their agreement with a hug.

They decided that Sir Quiggly Comear should be sent for. Final arrangements could now be put in place for the Royal Christening, and of course a huge party for all the people.

Sir Quiggly joined the happy family and was delighted with the chosen names. He thought they were both splendid and perfectly suitable for the future Artonian King.

There was only one cathedral and one bishop in Artonia. It was agreed that the ceremony should take place in two weeks' time. The ancient, but venerable Bishop Bjorn Toby Bishop would lead proceedings. This was a little worrying as the holy man was now ninety nine years old. He had become a tiny bit confused. He was however much loved by all the people. Nobody much minded if he got things a bit muddled from time to time.

There would be a parade after the service from the cathedral to the Royal Park. There a grand party would be held. There would be pink lemonade, strawberry shortbread, and in recognition of Her Majesty's love of fishing, fish finger sandwiches. To welcome the baby, and all the young children of Artonia there should be much bunting, candy floss and brightly coloured balloons.

Notices were sent out. The Artonians, who we already know like any excuse for a bit of a party, began to look forward to the new Prince's special day.

CHAPTER 8. THE CHRISTENING GETS CARRIED AWAY

The day of the christening was bright and sunny. What few clouds there were seemed to be floating like candy floss in a sea of blue sky. This was most excellent news for the crowds that had gathered to watch the parade. There was as predicted a lively party atmosphere. There were flags, different coloured gas filled balloons and parking ticket confetti. All Artonians like to throw confetti at every public occasions not just at weddings.

At 1.45 p.m. precisely the palace gates were opened and King Richard Ricardo and his wife Her Majesty Queen Flotilla appeared in their very best robes. The King had on his flamingo feathered crown and

Flotilla wore her special fisherman's smock. The young Prince Roland was in the family's vintage pram. This had been used for generations. It tilted slightly forward and had low sides. This meant that everybody could get a great view of the new heir to the throne as the royal party walked towards the cathedral. There was much cheering and waving, and shouts of;

"Well done Your Majesties!"

"Gooby gooby-goo your Princeliness! and a final.

"Good luck with Bishop Bishop!"

This last call was from a citizen of Artonia who knew from first-hand experience that the ancient clergyman was subject to some confusion in his later years. At his own wedding a few months earlier it had been third time lucky before he was actually married to his wife. Firstly the good Bishop had tried to marry the poor chap to his uncle Cyril. He had next tried to marry him to a fine statue of the late King Ringo Roscoe. Finally an very happily he marrried him to his wife!

They arrived at the cathedral after their brief procession. The congregation all applauded as the royal party walked to the altar. Bishop Bjorn Toby Bishop was waiting for them.

Silence fell on the assembly, as Bishop Bishop began.

"It is, with a heavy heart, that we meet today to say farewell to our beloved friend..." A junior clergyman stepped up quickly and whispered in the

Bishop's ear. He continued.

" Oh I am so sorry, I'll start again. Dearly beloved we are gathered here today to join together this man and this woman in holy matri..." The young clergyman stepped up and whispered again. "Is the wedding off then?" asked the Bshop.

At this point another young clergyman stepped up to the other ear. Both good gentlemen gently got the message across.

"Ah ha!" exclaimed Bishop Bishop. "Now I'm there. Now I'm there. Let us see our new Prince."

Flotilla scooped the baby up in her arms. He was wrapped tightly in a blanket with just his face peeping through. The Bishop took the baby carefully in his ancient hands. He turned him round and held him up for all the congregation to see.

At that very moment a cloud outside began to clear. This allowed the sunlight to burst through a high window on the side of the church. This caused the Prince to be lit up in a glorious beam of golden sunlight. This made him blink and turn his head slightly to one side.

Many in the cathedral gasped! To the people it looked as if the Prince had shone like gold and then winked at them. This, they thought, was a sign of good things to come. The gasp turned to murmurs as the baby was lowered once more into his adoring mother's arms. The Bishop said a number of special prayers and finally blessed him saying;

"I name this child His Excellency Prince Roland Reginald P. Nutt-Butter, son of our own King Richard Ricardo and his feisty wife Flotilla."

At this point things began to veer a little off course as he continued,

"May God bless her and all who sail in her. What is joined together, speak now or forever hold your peace be with you now and always. Amen. May I go and have a cup of tea now?"

The two younger clergymen stepped quickly in to help Bishop Bishop conclude the formal ceremony with some grace. He bowed to the King and Queen, wished them a long and happy marriage and left the altar.

The Prince was placed back in his pram. King Richard and Queen Flotilla headed down the main aisle. They pushed the pram with Prince Roly towards the great west door. The congregation clapped, and the crowds outside picking up on the happy noise began to cheer, applaud and generally make as much noise as they could.

As King Richard, the Queen and the baby emerged someone near the door shouted,

"Three cheers for Prince Roly, Hip Hip!" "Hooray"

"Hip hip!" "Hooray"

"Hip hip!" "Hooray"

At that moment a young girl of six or seven broke free from the crowd and ran forward to tie a bright red balloon to the front of the pram.

"Thank you my dear." said Queen Flotilla.

"A lovely gesture." said the King.

Not to be outdone another child from the other side of the roadway ran up and tied a blue balloon to the front of the pram.

"How kind." thanked the Queen.

"Delightful." smiled the King.

Two more children broke ranks one with a yellow and one with a green balloon.

"Isn't this jolly." said the Queen.

"Absolutely super." beamed the king.

All at once a veritable rainbow scrum of children ran forward. At least a dozen or more balloons were tied to the pram.

"Thank you, but I think that will do now children." said Flotilla. She was a little anxious that the commotion would upset the baby.

"Oh yes." said the King, "I think that's enough balloons for the little chap now children."

The children let go of the pram and scuttled back to their places in the crowd.

The Queen holding the pram firmly took a small step forward. As she did so the front wheels made a very tiny jump. The Queen paused. Suddenly both wheels made another little jump and then rose into the air. Slowly at first, but with gathering momentum the pram began to take off.

"I say!" said King Richard, "Look at it go!"

Her Majesty, who was holding the bar at the back of the pram was not so enthralled. As the pram continued to rise steadily into the air she held on tightly. She tried her hardest to bring it back safely to the ground. But no, it went straight up at a steady pace and in just a few seconds the pram, the Prince and the Queen were airborne.

"Richard!" screamed The Queen, "Do something."

The King turned and falling to his knees grabbed both of Flotillas ankles which were now some several inches off the ground. Things seemed to steady, but in only a moment His Majesty too began to rise. He tried to pull downwards, but the balloons were pulling upwards, and clearly with more success.

His Majesty pulled down.

The balloons pulled up.

His Majesty pulled harder.

The pram still rose.

The balloons were winning.

The Royal family were heading up, up and away!

Scudamore who as usual was in fretful attendance joined the skyward tug of war.

"It's all right Your Majesties! I'll get you down!" he called. He grabbed the King's legs holding on for all he was worth. The pram seemed to stutter, but then with a gentle breeze, set off once more ascending like a giant tailed four wheeled kite up and into the sky.

This had all happened in less than half a minute. The crowd had frozen, open-mouthed. Watching as if held in a trance. Finally one good citizen broke the spell, stepped forward and bellowed

"Come on everyone, we have to save the baby!" With that he grabbed Scudamore by his left leg. Our hero's feet were dragged along the ground a few steps, but he did not take off.

A few more good citizens then ran forward and joined the fray. There was much climbing and tugging. Feet went in ears, and knees on noses. But slowly the Artonian ballast began to win. The pram, The Prince, The Queen, The King, Scudamore, and all the rescuers came back to the earth with a firm but gentle bump.

Balloons were quickly untied and released to the air. There was then quite some minutes of the dusting of hands, the rubbing of sore ankles and the hugging and patting of backs. The adventure finally came to a happy conclusion. Her Majesty checked that the baby was okay, which indeed he was. Everyone breathed a huge sigh of relief. The King stepped forward.

"Well my word." he pronounced. "I do hope that not every day is quite so exciting for our young son. I am not sure about you my wonderful people, but I am famished…Flotilla?"

"Absolutely starving my dearest."

"Very well. Let us all continue to the Royal Park where I believe a most excellent tea awaits. Onward one and all."

There was another great cheer. With everyone now safely back on terra-firma the good people of Artonia joined Their Majesties. They took a gentle stroll to the park where the real celebrations joyously began.

The Prince was now variously being called, 'The Pilot Prince', 'Prince Rocket Roly' and 'The Airborne Heir'.

He slept contentedly through the rest of the morning.

CHAPTER 9   READ ALL ABOUT IT

Back at the Palace life began to settle into a more normal routine. The loving parents spent a great deal of time both caring for and entertaining their young son. He was now by popular agreement called quite simply 'Prince Roly.'

As with all new parents the King and Queen were anxiously watching and waiting for young Roly to pass some of those great milestones that every new infant must pass. The first smile. The first gurgle. The first laugh. The first sit up. The first crawl. The first step, The first word, and eventually the first successful use of the potty !

Just a few weeks after the christening the family were relaxing together in the nursery.

"Look Ricardillo! Roly is smiling." called Flotilla excitedly

" Are you sure dearest? That shouldn't happen for a month or so yet."

"Well you have a look."

"I think he looks a bit uncomfortable. Maybe the poor chap has a bit of wind."

So saying His Majesty picked young Roly up, put him over his shoulder and patted his back. The young Prince wiggled, giggled, burped and then sent a fair portion of milky sick down the King's back.

"Well done young chap!" said the King delightedly

"Oh!" sighed the Queen " I was certain it was a smile."

"There's no rush you know Flotsie. I was a very late developer in all areas apparently."

Her Majesty was in no way surprised at this information, but her love for the King kept her from commenting.

"I suppose I am just being a bit impatient my dearest." said the Queen.

"Perfectly normal I am sure, but we don't want Roly doing everything all at once do we? There would be nothing to look forward to." said the King wisely for once.

"And what about keeping the people informed Richard. They will want to know about their Prince Roly."

"But they do know about him. There were hundreds cheering him along at his christening parade, and even more who came to tea."

"I know they know about him, but they will certainly want to know more about him as more about him to know becomes known."

This sentence for the King was a bit like being hit over the head during a full blown pillow fight. Incidentally he and Her Majesty still enjoyed these fun fights from time to time. Although His Majesty had never managed to win one, yet!

"Well? Phwaw!" puffed the King, "I'm not sure I know about all this knowing about stuff. What are we talking about?"

"The people Richard will be keen to hear about Prince Roly's progress. When he starts smiling, eating solid food, sitting up, all that sort of thing."

"Ah ha! I get the picture…and that, my dearest is the answer. The people must get the picture. Indeed get all the pictures, as our Roly achieves these important milestones. I think this is a job for the Artonian National Times. What do you say my sweetheart?"

"That is a perfect solution Ricardillo. What a clever boy you are today."

Sir Quiggly Comear was asked to arrange a meeting at the palace with the editor, the chief reporter, the photographer and the owner of the Artonian National Times or 'ANTs' as it was lovingly known. These four impressive posts were all held by the same one person. She came in the energetic and excitable form of Miss Gloria 'Scoop' Da Loop. Miss Da Loop produced the weekly edition of ANTs which was in fact the nation's only newspaper. Your may think one edition per week might not seem quite enough for the country's only newspaper. However, to be honest, exciting news was sometimes a little hard to come by in Artonia.

Naturally enough events like the Prince's christening and the great balloon lift off called for many pages of photographs, comment and discussion. On other weeks however there was little that was newsworthy. Headlines could be hard to come by. On one week for example the best that could be managed was:
"ARTONIAN COW STUBS HOOF!"
Another that was perhaps even worse was:
" MAN GOES FOR WALK"

Gloria 'Scoop' Da Loop arrived at the palace on her favourite roller boots. She wore roller boots at all times so that she could get to anywhere that anything exciting was happening as soon as possible. She was always on the go, whizzing from one place to another. She took with her a notebook, her pencil and her very best camera slung carelessly over one shoulder. Gloria was quite a smallish person with a beaming smile and a great mop of fizzing red hair. This surrounded her head like a tangerine halo.

Sir Quiggly welcomed her, and together they went up the stairs to the royal nursery. Gloria tip-toed carefully so as not to roll backwards and take a tumble.

Sir Quiggly knocked and they entered the nursery.

"Your Majesties", he began "May I present Miss Gloria 'Scoop' Da Loop editor in chief of the Artonian National Times."

King Richard sprang up, took Gloria's hand and shook it vigorously. This caused her wonderful mop of hair to wobble gently like an indoor firework.

"I do love your hair " said Queen Flotilla breaking the ice, "Does it take you an age to get ready each day?"

"Oh no Your Majesty," replied Gloria, " It's always been like this ever since I was a child. Daddy used to call me his Ginger Dandelion."

"Well, it is very dandy." said the King, "Now please do take a seat Miss Da Loop."

Gloria sat down and surveyed the brightly coloured nursery with its trapezes, hoops, unicycles and other circus equipment.

"What an exciting room!" she exclaimed.

"For an exciting baby, we hope." said the Queen.

"It is about the Prince that we wish to talk to you Miss Da Loop."

"Great!" she said, "I am all ears."

"Are you?" puzzled the King, "It's hard to really tell with all that wonderful hair, but if you say so. Now to cut a long story short Miss Da Loop, we would like you to take care of our child. Watch his development and so forth and so on."

,

"Me!" gasped Gloria dropping her pencil and notebook, "But I don't know anything about babies. I'm a reporter, not a nanny!"

"I don't think His Majesty has explained himself too clearly," calmed the Queen, "What he meant was that we would like your newspaper to have exclusive access to report on the Prince's development. Maintain a watching brief as it were. Keep the people posted on how he's doing."

"Wow!" grinned Gloria "That is fantastic. I'll have something for the paper every week, that the people will really want to read."

Sir Quiggly butted politely in.

"I do believe the people might get rather bored if they read about Prince Roly every week. Their Majesties were thinking more of special events. When the young chap reaches a memorable milestone."

"Exactly!" added Queen Flotilla, "So when he has his first smile, or eats his first toast, or takes his first step we'll send straight for you."

"And when he first sits on the potty?" said Gloria a little carelessly out loud.

"We shall send for the housemaid." answered the Queen, cutting short the conversation.

"I would be more than honoured to accept this task Your Majesties," said Gloria making a small bow. This sent her hair once more into a sustained rhythmic wobble like a nodding toy at the back window of a car. "When would you like me to start?"

The King and Queen looked at each other and with a warm smile nodded in agreement.

"No time like the present." said the King.

"You had some excellent photographs of the christening. Maybe now the people would like a picture of Roly at home, here in his nursery with mum and dad."

Gloria blushed for a moment remembering the other photograph in that edition of ANT's. She had taken a photograph of the pram in flight. She had sat on the pavement to get a really good shot. The resulting picture had shown a great many legs and arms flying around in an unseemly manner. It looked a little like an octopus's disco.

"I hope you didn't mind my other picture? The one of the pram in flight?" Gloria asked.

"Certainly not," said the King, "It was our favourite. We would love a copy for the nursery wall so that we can tell Roly all about it as he gets a bit older."

Much relieved Gloria stood up and asked where they would like the photograph to be taken. It was agreed that in front of the trapeze with some other circus bits and bobs in view would be just perfect. Flotilla stood holding Prince Roly in her strong left arm. Richard trying to look very proud was standing to her right.

Gloria rolled back a few feet to the open nursery door to compose herself and her picture.

" This is great!" she called, "But I need to get some

more of those super paintings in, I'll just move back a foot or so."

So saying she rolled back gently all the time looking through the camera's viewfinder at the royal group. The staircase was behind her. Disaster was imminent. The King, the Queen and Sir Quiggly all called out in perfect unison:

"Do mind the…" too late… "Stairs!"

Gloria shot off the first step backwards. Her wheels scooted off step number two, then three and so on gathering momentum with a loud "KERDUNK" as she hit each step.

Doris Morris, the Royal Housekeeper, was at that very moment crossing the palace hallway. She was pushing a trolley laden with the week's laundry. Hearing the "kerdunking" sound she turned just in time to see Miss Da Loop hit the last step.

As she watched, the poor girl did a backwards somersault high up and through the air. Without a moment's thought or hesitation Doris shoved the trolley forward at some speed. It was perfectly timed to catch the flying reporter who fell deeply into the sheets and shirts with a muffled BMMPH!

After some minutes and some strong tea she recovered well enough to take the photograph. She was persuaded by all present to remove her roller boots until it is was time to go. She then set off safely back to her newspaper's offices to prepare the photograph and the story to go with it. This week's headline would not be so dull.

"YOUR FLYING REPORTER CATCHES ROYAL FAMILY AT HOME"

CHAPTER 10   SCHOOL, SURELY NOT

Prince Roly continued to flourish and grow with the loving care of his mother and father. Days and weeks ran into months and years. Unbelievably quickly he was just days away from turning five years old. The King's mind was full of cakes, candles and lemonade. The Queen however had other thoughts in her head.

She knew it would soon be time for the Prince to start at school. She also knew that His Majesty might find that idea a little bit hard to swallow.

At breakfast as the King was happily munching on some delicious pancakes with maple syrup, she decided to raise the subject. Roly was in the nursery practising his juggling.

"Ricardillo, I would like to talk about our son with you."

"Goodo! My favourite subject Flotsie." replied the King, quickly licking his sticky wicky lips and savouring every drop of the yummy syrup.

"Now Richard. You know that Roly was born five

years ago my dear."

"Yes dear of course. I was there. I remember. So were you."

This was not going to be easy.

"Yes Richard I was. But now Roly is all but five years old there is something we have to consider."

"I know." said the King, getting quite excited," What shall we write on the cake."

"Well yes," said the Queen "But there is something more important to consider."

"More important?"

"Yes."

"The icing?"

"No."

"The balloons?"

"No."

"Party games?"

"No Richard. I am thinking about after Roly's birthday. There is no easy way of saying this. It is time for him to start at school."

"School? Surely not! Roly is far too young!"

"Five is the starting age for school."

"Oh dear, oh dear!" said the King sadly with real tears forming in his eyes and drip-dropping on to his plate. The Queen rushed to comfort him, never expecting such a reaction. She wrapped her arms around him and spoke softly.

"There now Richard, school's not so bad. I think

Roly will have a great time, really."

"But it's really horrible. I hated it. Sent away for ten weeks at a time. Lessons, homework and no cuddles from Ma and Pa."

"Sent away! We're not sending Roly away, and I did not know that you were Richard."

"Well I don't like to talk about it. When you talk about something you have to remember it. It then pops back in your head like a nasty taste that you can't wash away."

"So where did you go?"

"A boarding school just for young royals in Sazbecisland. The teachers were okay, and some of the other princes and princesses were okay, but I just wanted to be at home with Ma and Pa. They thought it was the right thing to do. Lots of other royal children were sent there so they thought they should send me. I never complained, I thought it would upset them. I just longed for my holidays and then bit my lip when it was time to go back." The King sobbed.

"Oh my poor darling," said the Queen, herself getting very teary. "Listen Richard, listen. We shall never send our Roly away. He'll go to school here in Artonia. We will take him each day, and fetch him home in time for tea."

"Here? Really? Here! Oh that's wonderful news.

Here in the City?" said the much relieved King drying his eyes.

"Yes, with all the other boys and girls. He may be going to be King one day, but he's still a little person. He'll be best off with other little persons learning about life."

"Oh Flotsie, I do love you. Would you like a pancake?"

King Richard dried his eyes and celebrated this excellent news by consuming another three pancakes. He quite forgot that he was supposed to be sharing them with his beloved, wise and wonderful wife.

There was one school in Artonia which served all the children of the city and the surrounding villages. It was organised like a great big pizza. It was divided into 6 lovely slices, and each slice looked after a different ages of children. The first slice, let's call it the Margharita, was for the 5 and 6 year olds where Roly was to make a gentle start. Next was the Pepperoni for the 7 and 8 year olds with some more complicated bits. The older the children the more exotic the ingredients. The 15 and 16 year olds had the Grand Mega Chilli Feast with extra onions and jalapenos on their spicy slice!

Of course it wasn't all about eating, it was about

learning, friendship and fun.
It was a very happy school. Indeed the school motto was:
"Happy To Be Learning and Learning To Be Happy".

The Headteacher was one Quentin Buttercup, and it was this delightful man's equally lovely wife Mrs Betty Buttercup who was the teacher in charge of the first class. This is where the Prince was brought for his very first day in school.

King Richard and Queen Flotilla had both accompanied him. They stood outside the class door.
"Have you got your sandwiches?"
"Yes Mum."
"Have you got your snack?"
"Yes Dad."
"Have you got your indoor shoes?"
"Yes Mum."
"Have you got your sun hat?"
"Yes Dad." Roly was getting exasperated.
"Can we go in now. I don't want to be late on my first day."
The Queen spoke once more "Very well Roly. Now I don't want any tears my darling."
"I won't cry Mum, I'm a big boy now."
"I know Roly. I was talking to your father."

"I am all right." said the King biting hard on the

knuckle of his first finger. "I just have a little dust in my right eye. Hug Roly?"

"Bye Dad, see you later."

"Bye Roly, love you."

"Now Roly" you be the best boy, and have a lovely day." said the Queen.

"Bye Mum, love you…and you Dad."

With that Roly opened the door to the class and went very bravely in, all on his own.

The King dabbed his eyes and smiled at the Queen who took her husband's arm and steered them both back to the school gates where they had left their royal bicycles.

CHAPTER 11   A NEW FRIEND

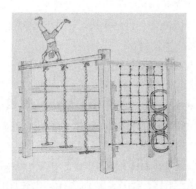

Prince Roly stepped into the class and was met by a huge burst of colour and sound. The calm and ship like shape of Mrs Buttercup sailed up before him. Smiling warmly she said hello and wrapped his hand in her warm soft fingers. They felt like newly baked bread. She led him across the room. The other children were all sat upon the floor and became very quiet and still as Roly and his teacher approached. Roly felt just a very slight flutter in his tummy as if a tiny little creature had started to dance down there.

"Now boys and girls, I want you all to say hello to our new boy Roly."

"Good morning Roly." they all said in one creaking chant.

"I want someone to look after Roly today, show him

the ropes, and I think that someone should be...
Boris Morris. Is that all right Boris?"
"Yes Mrs Buttercup."
"Right then everyone let's start our morning. Time to choose what you would like to do. Off we go."

Boris stared at Roly, and Roly stared back at Boris. Boris spoke.
"Are you really the King?"
"No. I'm just a Prince."
"That's all right then. Do you like digging?"
"I love digging."
"All right. Come with me."

Boris extended his left hand, which Roly took. Unlike the warm and fluffy fingers of Mrs Buttercup, Boris's fingers were hot and sticky like five well chewed toast soldiers smeared with honey. They felt good. Roly allowed himself to be tugged across to the huge sandpit. He and his new friend began to build a great big castle.

The minutes of the morning sped by as Roly and Boris moved quite freely from one activity to another. They went from the sand to water, from water to puzzles, from puzzles to dressing up and from dressing up to drawing.

The pair chattered and played and played and chattered. From time to time Mrs Buttercup would join them for a few minutes to make certain all was well. She would then move on to see how others were getting on.

At midday a little bell rang and everyone went to get their lunch boxes. The children sat in a large circle on the floor to eat their sandwiches, fruit, cakes and biscuits. Roly had cheese and pickle in his sandwich and a small flapjack that his father had especially made for him.on his first day at school.

While the children ate Mrs Buttercup read them a story about a sad dragon whose fire had gone out. A little boy from a nearby village had helped him get it back again. For the first time since the school day had started the children stopped their chattering and nattering, and became lost in the words of the story.

After half an hour of munching, listening and resting, the rest of the day began.

"To awaken ourselves for the afternoon children," began Mrs Buttercup, "We shall have some activity, and why dear children do we do that?"

"Because active children have active minds." chorused the class.

"Very good," said Mrs Buttercup "and we shall start as usual with a dance."

Roly loved to dance, and was always dancing at the palace with his mum and dad. The music Mrs Buttercup put on was very loud, very fast and very exciting. The boys and girls wiggled and waggled, hopped and bopped, bumped and jumped and rocked and rolled until with a big splash of sound the song ended. Everyone clapped each other and got their breath back for a moment.

"Well done everyone," praised Mrs Buttercup whose cheeks were now glowing a lovely warm pink.

"That was super dancing. You may now choose your own activity indoors or outside in the play area. Please all be careful and help one another. Off you go now."

"Shall we do some climbing?" asked Boris of his new friend

"I love climbing." said Roly, and they set off to the large climbing frame just outside of the classroom.

A few minutes later Mrs Buttercup was helping a group of five children who were trying to build themselves into the tallest pyramid they could. They kept collapsing into a muddled heap of arms, legs and giggles. Boris suddenly appeared at her side.

"Please Mrs Buttercup?"

"Yes Boris, what may I do for you?"

"I cannot get up as high as Roly. Will you help me please?"

"Certainly Boris, I'll be right out when I've untangled this little group." said Mrs Buttercup.

As Mrs Buttercup went outside the first thing she noticed was that there were about half a dozen children sitting on the floor staring up at the climbing frame and clapping. She turned and raised her eyes to see what it was that was holding the children's attention. She was more than surprised and not a little shocked to see that there, at the very top of the climbing frame, was the Royal Prince. He was standing on his two hands with his legs completing a near perfect ' X 'above him.

Mrs Buttercup took a big breath and calmed herself before speaking.

"Roly," she said clearly but gently, "Are you all right up there?"

Roly swung himself about in one movement and sat on the top-most bar of the frame with his arms folded in front of him.

"Yes thank you Mrs Buttercup."

"Um, I think it might be time to get down now Roly, move on to something else."

"Okay Mrs Buttercup. I'll come down." With that the heir to the throne stood up once more. He then proceeded to complete a perfect forward roll along the top bar. He next grabbed a rope to swing out over the play area. He let go and landed safely and at the feet of Mrs Buttercup. His audience clapped once more.

"Was that okay Mrs Buttercup?"

"Well yes Roly, that was fine. Tell me where did you learn to do all those twizzly balancing tricks?"

"Oh, that's my Mum. She's brilliant at those sorts of things. Dad tries too, but he tends to fall off." replied

young Roly.
"Right," said Mrs Buttercup whose heart was still beating quite a lot faster than normal. "Now for the last half an hour or so of the afternoon I would like you and Boris to go quietly into the class and to try and paint each other."

Boris smiled at his new friend and led him back into the classroom and the painting corner.
There followed a very happy half hour of mixing up paint and applying it to paper, cardboard, the tables but mostly each other. By the time the tidy up bell was rung both of the children looked like rainbow coloured parrots.

They were smothered with glorious thick paint on their hands, arms, faces and much of their clothing.
"Oh goodness," said Mrs Buttercup "I know I said paint each other but…well…never mind. Time to go home I think."
King Richard and Queen Flotilla were outside of the classroom door chatting with other parents. At first they did not recognise the brightly coloured bundle that ran towards them. Having finally realised that this living work of art was indeed their son they both hugged him tightly, sharing his paint between them.

"And how was your first day at school Roly?" asked his dad.

"Great," said the Prince "I've got a best friend called Boris. He's lovely."
"Wonderful." said the Queen, who took her son's hand.
The King and Queen spoke with Mrs Buttercup and thanked her for making Roly's first day such fun. She in turn decided not to mention the gymnastics display and commented instead on what a happy and polite young man His Majesty was.

A very proud mother and father led their son out of the school gates and back towards the palace for tea.

CHAPTER 12   DOUBLE FIGURES

Roly loved his school, and over the next few years he began to grow and flourish. He really excelled at all things physical. If it needed lifting, climbing, running or throwing Roly was there. He would be lifting higher, climbing more swiftly, running faster and throwing further. He was a natural when it came to anything sporty.

When it came to work that was, shall we say, more 'bookish', the young Prince was not quite so keen. He had inherited his father's rather strange approach to thinking and problem solving.

This meant that he often arrived at somewhere close to a sensible answer. However his was achieved by his brain following a long and often bizarre journey to heaven knows where and back again.

Roly, along with all the other children in his class, had to take small tests on occasion to see how he was doing. His answers whilst being very imaginative were sometimes a little off the mark. A few examples might illustrate the point:

Question. What are two twos? - Ballerina's dresses.
Question. What is the opposite of if? - Niff.
Question. When was Shakespeare born?- On his birthday.
Question. What is a polygon? - An escaped parrot.

When King Richard visited the school on "Progress Evenings" he looked at his beloved son's answers to such test questions. He was delighted at how well he was doing. He saw nothing odd himself in the boy's responses. Her Majesty Queen Flotilla was also delighted because it was her husband's offbeat thinking that had helped her to fall so quickly in love with him. She could see that their son had also been blessed with the same cross-wired brain patterns. This filled her with happiness and confidence for his future happiness.

His best friend remained Boris Morris the boy who had helped him on his first day. The two were inseparable.

As it turned out Boris's mum was Doris Morris who worked in the palace. Boris would come over with his mum to play at the palace while she was working and Roly would visit the Morris family to play there. Boris had a lively dad called Horace and a brother and sister called Norris and Florris. They were twins. Floris being born 5 minutes after her brother was called Floris Morris Minor.

The two boys would play the most marvellous games that would sometimes last for days. They were forever fighting dragons, flying to the moon or chasing baddies.

It was soon to be Prince Roly's birthday and at last he was reaching double figures. Ten years old in just over a week. He was with his parents early one school morning eating some creamy porridge with honey and banana.

"You know that it's my birthday next week Mum and Dad?"

"Yes Roly," said his father "Ten years ago since you swam into the world."

"Well, I don't want to have a party this year."

"No party!" said the King "But I love your parties Roly. They're great fun with all those games, prizes and dressing up."

This was true, the King loved the parties so much that Flotilla really wondered who the parties were for, Roly or his Dad.

"Yes, well I do love them too Dad, but I would like to do something different this year. Especially as I am going to be ten. That's double figures.".

"Oh" grizzled His Majesty

"Don't get grumpy dearest." said the Queen catching King Richard's attention before the grump turned into a sulk. "It is after all Roly's birthday, not yours or mine."

The King snapped quickly out of his mood.

"You are of course as ever quite right my dear." He smiled warmly at his young son "Well Roly what would you like to do on your birthday?"

"Well Dad. I would like to go camping…"

Before he could finish this sentence his dear darling father's imagination had leapt into action. He and Roly with sturdy boots and laden rucksacks were heading into the mountains. With them a tent, some sleeping bags and a compass. Wild animals were stalking their every move (mountain goats actually). Great birds of prey were watching them from on high.

"What a great adventure we shall have Roly. Father and son alone in the mountains using their wits to survive."

"Not with you Dad !"

You could almost hear the King's bubble going "Pop!"

"I want to go with Boris. And not in the mountains, in the meadow next to the palace farm."

The palace did indeed have a small piece of land next to an old barn. This was sufficient to keep a few Artonian Blue Cows (3 to be exact) and a dozen or so hens. Between them kept the palace in milk, cheese and eggs.

The King was beginning to sink with disappointment. His wife threw him a lifeline.

"Your bottom lip is about to hit the floor Richard. Haul it back in please. I think it is a marvellous idea Roly. You and Boris can go down to the meadow next Saturday in the morning to set up your camp. Your father and I will come and visit your camp at tea-time with a birthday picnic. Mr and Mrs Morris can come along too and Norris and Floris. We will then leave you in peace for the rest of the night. How does that sound Roly?" said his Mum.

"Great Mum. Is it all right with you Dad?"

King Richard's spirits had bounced up once more. Already he was a planning a picnic full of surprises. "Oh yes Roly, splendid, totally splendid. What a clever chap you are for thinking of it."

With that the family all carried on with the rest of their day and began to plan for the great adventure the following week.

Boris arrived at the palace at 8 o'clock on the Saturday morning of Prince Roly's tenth brthday.

The two boys hurried up to Roly's room to get ready.

"I've got the tent." said Roly

"I've drawn a map." said Boris

"Wow ! A map. That's really cool. Show me Boris."

They studied the map which Boris had drawn. On it was the palace, the gardens, the farm, the old barn. Just beyond it was the meadow which nestled between the farmyard and a small wood that skirted around the far edge of the palace grounds.

"We need to go this way." explained Boris who had used bright yellow dots to show the route they would take, zigzagging their way to the meadow.

"That looks great Boris. You lead and I'll follow okay?"

"Fine" said Boris. " Now, have we got everything Roly. We ought to check before we set off."

"Okay Boris," replied Roly standing to attention and pretending to salute. In their games and adventures it was almost always Boris who took control of organising things or making up good rules. For Roly that was just fine because it was playing the games that he enjoyed and not all that 'sorting out' business. Boris was really good at taking charge and explaining things. Neither found it odd that the future king should be the one following rules and taking orders and not the other way round. They never gave it a thought.

"Sleeping bags?" started Boris.

"Check." replied Roly.

"Compass?"

"Check."

"Torches?"

"Check."

"Water bottles?"

"Check."

"Pyjamas?"

"Check check!" said Roly

"Check check?" asked Boris a bit puzzled

"Yes check check…I've got my yellow and blue checked pyjamas so it's check check and that's check mate!"

Both of the friends fell about laughing. King Richard and Queen Flotilla arrived at Roly's door and were greeted by the sound of happy laughter.

"All ready then you two?" asked the Queen.

"Yes Mum. Boris has double checked everything!"

That started them both giggling again.

"Are you sure you don't want a hand carrying some of this lot boys?" asked the King quite hopefully.

"No thank you Your Majesty." said Boris politely "My Dad found two old rucksacks in the attic. Everything will fit in those. We'll manage."

"Please remember boys that you may build a bonfire, and we will light it when we come down with the picnic. Is that okay?"

"Yes Mum, that sounds great."

"That's my boy." said the King. "Now I think you two had better get going, or the day will be done and dusted."

With that the boys packed up their rucksacks and put them on their young shoulders. The rucksacks were quite large adult ones. As the boys went down the stairs they looked a little like two hermit crabs scuttling down some rocks towards the sea.

"Are you sure you'll be okay?" called the King from the landing.

"Daaaaad!" called Roly, "We'll be fine."

And so saying the two adventurers exited through the front doorway of the palace.

King Richard looked anxiously at the Queen.

"Do you think they'll be all right my dearest?" he asked.

"Richard, they're only going to the meadow, they'll be there in no time. Now stop worrying, and go and help Boris's Mum in the kitchen. You've got cakes to bake."

The King was suitably, re-assured and distracted. He slid royally down the bannisters and went into the kitchen to help Doris Morris with preparations for the birthday picnic.

CHAPTER 13   THE ADVENTURE BEGINS

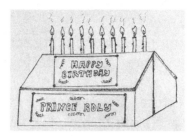

Prince Roly and his best friend set off through the palace gardens following the zigzag route that Boris had drawn up on his map. Every hundred metres or so they would stop, take their rucksacks off their shoulders, sit down and consult the map. They would check the compass directions and with the help of an old pair of binoculars decide upon their next target destination. They would then set off once more. Roly was continually leaping ahead and peering round suspicious bushes and trees as if expecting to find a wild animal or other unwanted visitor lurking there.

"Tell me again Boris why we are following this map to the meadow instead of just walking straight there?" asked the Prince.

"Because," began Boris "If we went straight there it would only take us about ten minutes and we would think we were still at home."

"But we are still at home aren't we?"

"I know Roly, but it's all part of the adventure. It make it feel as if we've gone on a longer journey." explained Boris.

"But we will have gone a lot further but be no further away." said Roly.

"You are absolutely right Roly, but sometimes how you get somewhere is far more important than where you get to."

The puzzled Prince was not too sure what his friend was trying to explain to him, but he trusted him completely. He knew that Boris usually got things right. He was happy to zig and zag and zag and zig as much as was needed.

After more than an hour and a half they arrived at the meadow.

"Wow!" said Roly " I am exhausted. That was quite some journey Boris."

"It was Roly, but we did well and didn't get lost once. We've done really well."

"Have we?" beamed Roly "That's good news, and now we are here."

"Yes indeed we are Roly, and we better get sorted. First things first, we need to put the tent up."

"Leave that to me Boris. I'll have that done in a jiffy."

Boris sat on the grass with his back against a small plum tree to watch the show. He guessed it might not go quite as easily as Roly was hoping.

First of all Roly emptied out all of the poles, pegs, ropes and then the tent itself. Then there began a great deal of moving one pole from A to B and another from B to C and yet another from C to D and so on. Before long the entire alphabet had been used up, but little progress was visible. Ropes were tied and untied, arms and legs got wrapped in canvas. Eventually there was one glorious giant mess with Prince Roly in its centre trying to get the tent to stand up as it should. He was huffing and puffing, and grunting and groaning. Eventually he collapsed in a heap with the tent all around him. Its poles and ropes were spread out like some giant canvas squid.

"It's no good Boris" said Roly, " They must have given me the wrong poles and ropes for this tent. It just will not fit together."

"Let me have a go." said Boris.

Roly climbed up into the branches of the little plum tree and sat in a shady spot while his friend had his turn at putting up the tent.

Boris first opened the tent fully out into a large rectangle, with its edges all around it. He clipped a few poles together and tucked them in each of the four corners and laid one long pole right down the middle. He tied a few ropes together, pegged them in to the ground, then attached them to the four poles. Finally by pulling one rope the whole tent stood up straight and true. A last peg was banged firmly into the ground and the tent was up, ready, proud and perfect.

"Well," said Boris "Aren't you going to come and

look inside?!

Roly swung down from the branch and in one fluid move landed at his friend's feet.

"That was brilliant Boris. I knew we'd do it in the end."

With that the two boys dragged the rest of their equipment into the tent and sorted out everything they would need for their stay.

The afternoon was spent climbing trees, collecting firewood, playing hide and seek (which Roly never seemed to win) and enjoying the warm sunshine of the meadow. Although in clear sight of the palace they were blissfully alone and enjoying their adventure.

Towards the end of the afternoon the boys spotted the picnic procession heading down through the palace gardens. There was King Richard, Queen Flotilla, Doris Morris and her husband Horace with the Morris twins Norris and Floris.

Following on a few metres behind was Sir Quiggly Comear and Scudamore. Behind them was the editor, journalist and photographer from ANT's, Miss Gloria 'Scoop' Da Loop. She had come to join in the celebrations, and take lots of photographs for next week's paper.

After a range of hugs, hellos and a few 'get off Dad's' rugs were spread on the ground and the grand birthday picnic set out for all to enjoy.

There were ham and jam sandwiches, (different

sandwiches that is, not with both fillings!) strawberry tarts, chocolate chip muffins, cold pizza slices, blueberry cookies, homemade lemonade and hazelnut meringues. Silence reigned as the feast was devoured.

When everyone thought they were full up King Richard opened a large box which contained a tent shaped cake, with ten candles dotted down its centre. Queen Flotilla lit the candles then Roly took an enormous breath and blew them all out. He did this a little too quickly for Miss Gloria 'Scoop' Da Loop who was trying to photograph the event. She asked very politely if he could do it once more which of course Roly was delighted to do. Everyone then sang Happy Birthday to Roly followed by three enormous hip-hip hoorays led by his Mum and Dad.

They then decided to all have a game of hide and seek.

Queen Flotilla was chosen to be seeker and had to count to 100 before going out to search for the others. Roly and King Richard were the first to be found. They had both chosen different ends of the same small bush to hide behind. This meant that their royal bottoms both stood out from either side of the bush and they were easily spotted.

The last to be found was Sir Quiggly. He had lain down behind a large fallen oak tree. After such a rich tea on so warm an afternoon he had nodded off and was soundly asleep. Everyone was called upon to look for the elderly gentleman. The King feared Sir Quiggly might have got lost in the woods. He was only found when he started snoring really loudly. The sound was amazing, much like a pig squealing on a roller coaster, if you can imagine such a thing.

The bonfire was then carefully lit. Sitting around its bouncing flames everyone was required to share their best joke, story or song. King Richard tried to tell a joke about a cowboy wearing brown paper trousers and a brown paper shirt who was arrested for rustling. He got a little muddled however and said cattle stealing instead of rustling. But everyone laughed as they knew the punch-line anyway. The King told the same joke at least two or three times a year, at Christmas and on birthdays.

As it began to get dark Queen Flotilla announced that it was time for everyone except the two boys to return to the palace. The fire was safely dampened down until completely out.

The boys could be left to enjoy the rest of their camping adventure on their own. There were more hugs, farewells and 'get off Dads' then at last the boys were able to settle down for the night.

CHAPTER 14 FELLUMP, FELLUMP, FELLUMP!

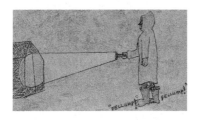

When the grown ups had all left the boys went into the tent. They climbed into their sleeping bags and got ready to go to sleep. Of course they couldn't, because they were still far too excited and wide awake. They decided therefore to tell each other a ghost story. Roly began by telling the story of one of his ancestors.

"Centuries ago he had managed, by accident, to lock himself in a dark and dusty corner of the palace's ancient cellars. He starved to death before either of his sons had found him. His ghost claimed Roly now roams the palace grounds looking for the two boys to punish them for not finding him sooner."

"Is that true?" asked Boris

"I don't know. Someone at school told me the story. I have never asked my Dad about it. I guess it was probably made up trying to scare me. Your turn Boris."

Boris began a tale about a statue of a wicked King.
"He had been really cruel to his people all through his life. Even after his death they were too scared to get rid of his statue even though they hated it. One day a brave boy called Boris, who was scared of nothing decided to destroy the statue. He went to the city square in the middle of the night with a big hammer. He raised it high over his head to strike it but as he did so something awful happened."

"What, what?" asked Roly, his eyes as wide as saucers. Boris continued with his story.

"Just as the hammer was coming down on the statue the old wicked King roared into life. He jumped down and chased the boy out of the city. He was never seen again. The statue was back in its usual place the next morning and the wicked King had an even more evil smile on his cold bronze face."

"Surely that cannot be true." said Roly "Statues can't come to life."

"How do we know Roly? We weren't there, and my Dad told me that story."

"Gosh."

"Mind you, if you tell a ghost story it is supposed to be scary. I guess it would be no good telling it and then saying it wasn't true. Would it?"

" I guess not." said the Prince." But I really hope it wasn't true!"

It was now really late and the weary boys finished their stories and drifted off to sleep.

Back in the palace an hour or so later King Richard was wide awake.

"But what if there are wolves?" he said.

"Darling Ricardillo there haven't been wolves in Artonia for over two hundred years."

"Yes, but that could change tonight."

"Don't be silly. Go back to sleep."

There was about thirty seconds of silence.

"There could be snakes you know, poisonous snakes."

"There are no poisonous snakes in Artonia Richard."

"It could have escaped from a zoo in another country and slithered over the mountains to get here hungry for fresh…I can't bear it."

"Now you are being very silly Richard. There are no snakes, no wolves and come to think of it no lions, no tigers and no llamas."

"I didn't know llamas were dangerous!"

"They are not! Oh Richard for goodness sake I am tired and I want to get some sleep!"

"But I can't sleep. I am worried about the boys."

"Then for heaven's sake, get up, put on a coat and some boots and go and check on them for yourself. It will only take a few minutes. You can put your mind to rest then come back to bed to get some sleep."

"Good idea as ever Flotsie."

"And Richard" continued the Queen "When you get

back to the palace do not, and I repeat, DO NOT, wake me up!"

"Right oh Flotsie. Back soon! But you won't know I'm back because I'll be so quiet. I will hardly breathe and you will not hear a..."

"Richard! Just go!"

Sensing the danger in the tone of those last three words the King left the royal chambers and went quietly downstairs. He had of course forgotten his coat and boots. However he thought it best not to return to the bedroom. Luckily on the stand by the front door was the big hooded coat that belonged to one of the palace gardeners. His wellingtons were right next to it. The King decided it would be a good idea to borrow the gardener's things for his expedition rather than venturing back upstairs.

He slipped softly out of the front door into the night. He was pleased to find that there was some light from a partially hidden moon to help him see where he was going. He was also pleased to find a torch in the gardener's coat pocket. He switched it on and set off through the gardens towards the farm and the meadow.

He tried to keep quiet, but the boots being a few sizes too big kept slipping off his feet. Each time he took a step they made a loud "fellumping" sound.

Coming past the farm and to the edge of the meadow he could see the outline of the tent and all was quiet.

"That all looks okay," thought the King to himself

"But how do I know the boys are in there and all okay? I'll get a little closer and see if I can hear them breathing."

He moved slowly closer with the "fellumping" sound of his footsteps echoing even more loudly as he approached the tent and the woods.

Inside the tent Boris woke up.

"Fellump!... Fellump!...Fellump!" he heard.

"What's that?" whispered Boris slightly startled.

Prince Roly woke up.

"What's what?"

"Listen!"

"Fellump!...Fellump!...Fellump!"

"Goodness," whispered Roly "Whatever is that?"

"Shush Roly. Maybe it will go away."

"Fellump!...Fellump!...Fellump!"

Outside the King stopped. He thought he could hear voices from within the tent. He decided to speak, but his voice came out in a strange and very gruff sort of whisper.

"Boys, boys...I've come looking for you, are you in there?"

"It's your ancestor's ghost!" said Boris.

"It's that evil statue come for more boys!" said Roly.

"Let's have a peek out of the tent door."

They inched the tent flap apart and peered into the darkness. There was a light shining straight at them and behind the light was a tall hooded figure with very large feet.

"It's the statue!"

"It's your ancestor!"

"Either way " said Roly "I don't like it. Come on Boris. When I say so we'll charge at it and scare it away."

"Okay Roly. I'm with you. Make a lot of noise too. That should do it."

The King spoke again in his strained whisper.

"Boys it's me...shall I come closer?"

"Now!" shouted Roly and throwing the tent flaps wide open both boys shot out of the tent screaming "CHARGE!" at the tops of their voices. They ran as fast and as hard as they could towards the ghostly apparition.

The King managed only a brief squawk as the two speeding boys hurtled into him. With shoulders down and arms outstretched they knocked the King flat on his back with a perfect rugby tackle.

"Oooof!" spluttered the King with all of the wind knocked out of his tummy.

Roly sat on the strange figure's chest. Boris sat on its knees. Roly saw the torch that had been knocked out of the creature's hands lying on the ground next to him. He picked it up.

"Right, now!" said the Prince "Let's see what you are."

He turned the torch to shine straight on the face of ...his father.

"Dad!" yelled Roly

"It's your Dad!" shouted Boris turning to look at him too.

The King tried to get his breath back as the boys climbed off him and helped him to stand up.

"Ah, well, I just popped down to see if all was all okay and er… I can see… that it is." stumbled the King.

"What did you do that for Dad?"

"Because I'm a silly old goat who loves his son very much, and I wanted to make sure he and his friend were okay. That's all Roly. I am sorry, I just couldn't help myself. I have also learned that you are not only all right, but that you and young Boris are both perfectly capable of looking after yourselves. I have the bruises to prove it."

Roly gave his Dad a big hug, then stepped back.

"It's okay Dad. Thanks for checking up on us. Sorry if we hurt you."

"Sorry Your Majesty" echoed Boris.

"My fault entirely boys. Now get yourselves back to sleep, and I'll get back to the palace. Night – night."

The boys got back into their sleeping bags and giggled softly to each other as they listened to his father slowly 'Fellumping' steadily back towards the palace.

CHAPTER 15 THE GREAT RACE

His Majesty King Richard had learned a good lesson that night. Over the next few years he kept his protective feelings at bay as best he could. He allowed his son more and more independence. Prince Roly repaid that growing trust by never breaking it. The bond between the boy and his father grew stronger and stronger. Her Majesty Queen Flotilla watched their relationship develop with great delight. Her husband and son meant the world to her and their happiness simply added to her own. Having said that they could still drive her to distraction, and more often than not did!

When Roly was nearly eighteen roller blading became a big craze amongst teenagers in Artonia. Roly had been taught to use roller boots when just six years old by Miss Gloria 'Scoop' Da Loop.

She always wore her roller boots. She had noticed how much the young Prince had seemed to admire them when visiting the palace for a photo-shoot. So on his sixth birthday she gave him a pair. With the permission of a delighted King and Queen she taught him how to ride them safely.

About a dozen years later roller blades came on the scene. These were all about speed, and Prince Roly was very fast. His father had taken up 'blading' as well, but he gave up after he had a couple of hair raising near misses. One involved a cow and a tractor, the other had involved poor Sir Quiggly and a coat stand. This had left a very painful impression on the elderly gentleman and a nasty impression on His Majesty's bottom. He decided to take Her Majesty's advice that roller-blading was really a young man's sport.

One bright spring morning Roly had gone across the city to see his best friend. Boris did have some roller blades, but was more interested in their design than actually riding on them. Boris had continued to do well at school, and loved anything to do with science and engineering in particular. The shed at the back of his house had become Boris's workshop. He was always in there tinkering with something and adapting it or building and designing something new.

"Hi Boris," said the Prince zooming up to the shed door and screeching to a halt. "Do you want to come blading."

"Maybe Roly, but can I show you something first?"
"Of course you can professor. What have you made this time?"
"Here it is, my new super streamline dyna-blade boot."
"Great name Boris, but they look like your old boots." said Roly.
The boots were indeed Boris's old ones. Boris explained however, that he had put special bearings inside the wheels, and a different shaped arch under the foot. These changes helped you stay up straighter when at speed.
"I reckon they will give you another couple of kilometres per hour easy."
"Wow Boris, they sound great. May I try them out?"
The boys had the same size feet, so that was not a problem. Roly was soon whizzing up and down the road, hollering with joy.
"Waaahooooo!" he screamed as he shot past Boris for the third time before pulling up quickly. "These are amazing Boris. I almost took off."
"That'll be my next invention then, jet powered roller blades and a winged jacket!"
Laughter as ever overtook them and they fell into a fit of giggles.
"But seriously Roly," said Boris recovering himself. "I reckon you could win the Round The Houses Race with those boots."
"What's the Round The Whatsits race then Boris. I've not heard about that?"

"It was advertised in today's ANT's. Miss Gloria 'Scoop' Da Loop has organised a roller-blading race through the city's streets. It's next Sunday."

"That sounds like great fun. I will go straight home and ask if its okay with Mum and Dad. Are you going to enter Boris?"

"No thanks Roly. I am happy being the engineer, you can be the test pilot!"

Later back at the palace his parents were excited at the prospect of the race.

"Of course you can enter Roly," said His Majesty. "And so will I."

"Richard!" interrupted Her Majesty.

"Err...And so will I be...er... there, with your mother, to cheer you on."

"Thanks Dad. Thanks Mum."

"Now Roly," said the Queen "You must not get too excited. I know you are jolly fast, but you may not win. You must remember that you are the future King of Artonia and behave in the correct way."

"You mean by having anyone who beats me thrown into the palace dungeons?"

"Roly!" exclaimed both his parents together.

"Just joking Mum and Dad. I honestly don't care if I win or not. It should just be a really fun day."

"That's the right spirit Roly." said his father. "I am always been able to lose with dignity."

"That is because you have had so much practice dear." teased his wife with a loving smile.

"I had better go and practice." said the Prince leaving his parents and going out once more on his roller-blades.

Once Roly was out of earshot Queen Flotilla spoke to her husband.

"Well done for not saying anything Ricardillo."

"What didn't I say anything about?"

"You know Ricardillo. When Miss Da Loop called this morning."

"Did she? Is she racing?"

"No Richard, she spoke about the trophy. She asked if we might present it to the winner of the race."

"Good job I am not racing then. I should not present myself with a trophy."

"Quite right," said his wife herself now totally confused, "But you could present it to Roly if he won."

"How grand that would be." said King Richard with a warm smile.

Their Majesties bustled through the next few days with growing anticipation at the forthcoming race."

The route for the race had been carefully planned to criss-cross the city visiting nearly every street. Stewards were placed along the route to keep an eye on the competitors and to help make sure the spectators stayed safely on the pavements.

The race was to start and finish on the same spot. This was great news for the King and Queen because they would be able to cheer for their son both at the start and finish of the race.

There were thirty brave souls who had entered the race and each wore a number on their shirts. Roly was number nine, which Boris said was his lucky number.

"Well I hope that doesn't mean I'll come ninth!" said Roly.

"Of course not Roly," Boris reassured him. "Now don't forget your race plan. What do you have to do at the post office?"

"Buy a stamp?"

"No, you don't buy a stamp. You begin to speed up for the last kilometre. Really and you'll lick the opposition."

"Yuk! I would rather lick a stamp."

"Lick the opposition means to beat them Roly. Look, just enjoy yourself okay."

"Will do Boris. You just watch me whizz."

Gloria blew a whistle to get everyone lined up for the start. She took the official race photograph first, then wished everyone good luck. She raised her hand holding a small flag and began a countdown, which the whole the crowd joined in with.

"10,9,8,7,6,5,4,3,2,1…Go!"

Everybody cheered as the bladers set off. The pace was really quite quick. To begin with all thirty racers moved ahead in one tight group. After about five minutes a small group of half a dozen moved ahead of the others. Roly was a part of this faster breakaway group and was doing well. The route went this way and that across the city and back. The crowds clapped and yahooed as the racers shot by.

At last Roly spotted the post office up ahead.

"Do I have to stop and buy a stamp?" he pondered "No, I remember. I have to speed up. We're getting close to the finish."

With that small thought safely in place Roly began to speed up. He went like a rocket and within a few seconds had created quite a lead for himself.

He was just thinking what fun the whole event was when, as he turned a final corner, up in the distance he saw a banner across the road. He knew that the banner was the finishing line. So he put his head down and really pushed hard.

Right next to the finishing line straining to see the racers approach was a little girl called Maisie. She was holding on tightly to her puppy Sproglet. The crowd were getting noisy which frightened poor Sproglet. The puppy began to wriggle, and then slipped out of Maisie's hands. It scampered straight into the middle of the road and the oncoming bladers. Maisie ran out after Sproglet. Seeing this the crowd gasped a united "No!"

Roly, who was being hotly chased by the rest of the group heard the gasp. He lifted his head just in time to see the little girl picking up her puppy just a few feet in front of him.

In a split second he braked, swivelled left to right and span round. In the same single movement he grabbed Maisie and Sproglet and swept across to the pavement and safety. The crowd cheered as the rest of the racers shot by them to cross the finishing line.

Maisie and Sproglet were safe, but Roly had lost.
The other racers realised what had happened. They went back to where Roly was standing. The winner of the race was called Lulu, she spoke first.

"The trophy is yours Your Majesty you won it fair and square." Everybody clapped in approval.
"Not at all," replied Roly "You crossed the line first you are the winner. I am happy that I just managed to stop these two from having a nasty bump. I have had a fabulous time. Please, go and get your trophy."

With that Prince Roly started to clap.
The rest of the crowd joined in and a smiling Lulu, turned and walked over to collect her winner's trophy. The King and Queen were waiting for her.
"Very well done young lady," said His Majesty.
"Good to see the girls doing so well," added the Queen.
"Thank you Your Majesties," said Lulu as she proudly took her trophy and having bowed a royal bow, turned and held up the prize.

The crowd cheered, Prince Roly and the other racers cheered, and the King and Queen clapped loudly. They also smiled warmly towards their beloved son feeling full of pride and love.

Miss Gloria 'Scoop' Da Loop caught the whole drama on camera and already had a headline in her thoughts.

**"LULU WINS THE RACE AND
PRINCE ROLY SAVES THE DAY"**

CHAPTER 16   THE OLYMPIC CHALLENGE

A short while after all the excitement of the 'Great Race' a letter arrived at the palace for the attention of Sir Quiggly Comear the King's Chief Advisor. It was from the International Olympic Committee. It invited Artonia to enter contestants for the Olympic Games which were this year being held in London, England.

Artonia had in fact only entered anyone for an Olympic event once, and that was some 24 years previously. Ivan Elovathro had taken part in the javelin competition. Unfortunately Ivan had been disqualified when, no doubt due to nerves, he threw his javelin in the wrong direction. It narrowly missed a group of spectators before spearing a king-size burger at the fast food outlet next to the main scoreboard.

Sir Quiggly was a much younger man then, and had to use all his charm and diplomacy to calm the officials down. They thought it had been a deliberate attempt to bring the games into disrepute. He shuddered at the memory.

Sir Quiggly was just about to put the forms into his waste paper bin when something caught his eye. It read:

"Event 74 [new event] 10 Kilometre Roller-Blade Race."

In a dusty corner of Sir Quiggly's aging brain he began to recall a similar race that had taken place in the city just a few weeks earlier. He asked his assistant Scudamore to help put him in the picture.

"So Prince Roly would have won the race then?" enquired Sir Quiggly after Scudamore had described the events of the day.

"Oh yes," explained Scudamore, "He was winning by a huge distance when he stopped to help the little girl and her dog."

"Well, I suppose we should ask the winner first, but I fancy we might have a royal candidate for the London Olympics. What do you think Scudamore?"

"I think it's a brilliant idea. Please allow me to speak to Lulu the winner of the race. I'll report back to you as quiggly as I can Sir Quickly... I mean...well...I'll just go" said a rather over excited Scudamore.

Lulu was one hundred per cent behind the idea of Prince Roly representing Aertonia in the Olympic race. The idea was then put before Their Majesties for approval which they duly gave.

When Prince Roly was asked if he would like to compete in the race his enormous "Yaaa... hoooooo!" could be heard in every room of the palace.

"Brilliant, brilliant, brilliant," he said. "I would love to do the race. Oh and by the way, what is an Olympics?"

After all had been explained to him Roly dashed off to meet with his best friend Boris to tell him the good news. Back in the royal apartments plans were being discussed.

"So where will Roly stay when he's in London?" asked Queen Flotilla

"I understand that all the competitors stay in a special athletes' village Your Majesty." explained Sir Quiggly.

"But he's a Prince for goodness sake, I am sure his cousin the Queen would want him to stay with her." said King Richard.

"Now Ricardillo," interrupted Flotilla. "Her Majesty Queen Elizabeth II is a very, very distant cousin. There has been no contact between the two families for years. The last contact was made by your great, great, great, great grandfather Roxy Renee. You told me that he sent his then already extremely distant cousin George the Third a get well card. He had heard he'd gone a bit off target in the thinking department."

"That'll be a family trait then." muttered

Scudamore just a little absent-mindedly.

"Beg pardon Scudamore, did you say something?" asked the King.

"Ah...I said er...that will be family all right then. The link's still there."

"Exactly. My point entirely. Sir Quiggly what do you think?" said King Richard.

"I think," responded Sir Quiggly as quickly as he could. "I think we should write to Her Majesty at Buckingham Palace and let her know of Prince Roly's attendance at the Games. Let her reply as she sees fit."

Flotilla thought that this was a fair arrangement and it would at least stop her husband from twittering on for hours and hours.

At Buckingham Palace when the letter was received, it was passed to an under-under-secretary to the Queen's under-secretary's assistant under-secretary's assistant to deal with.

He researched the Artonian dynasty's link to the British Royal Family. After hours of wading through endless dusty books of family trees he established that there had been some slight connection.

This was very, very slight and had occurred some centuries before. He checked through the book of Protocol and Manners that such a letter required for its answer. It became apparent that the Prince and his companions should indeed be offered accommodation as a guest of Her Majesty. However there was no requirement for there to be any meeting between Her Majesty and Prince Roland. In fact Her Majesty need not, and was not, ever informed of Prince Roly's purpose, visit or stay.

Sir Quiggly opened the letter from Buckingham Palace and noted that: "Her Majesty would be delighted to offer the Prince and his party residence at Windsor Castle throughout their stay.
Her Majesty regretted however that due to state responsibilities throughout the summer she would be unable to actually meet with him."
King Richard was delighted. Flotilla thought it was all a bit too much and that Roly would be better off with the other athletes. However she allowed her husband's family pride and joy to rule the day.
Roly began his training with real purpose. Boris helped him by designing his practice schedule and setting him daily targets. He also fine-tuned his roller blades helping to ensure the Prince would be at his very best for the race.
The next few weeks were very busy making sure everything was ready for the trip to London.
The Prince was expected to be accompanied by a team coach and a team doctor. Boris was quite naturally appointed as his coach. The the esteemed Doctor Erroneous Doodle, was invited to travel with the Prince as team doctor. The good medic had looked after the Prince since the day he was born, helping him through all of his childhood

ailments. He was delighted to be asked. Not least because it meant he would be travelling to London where he had studied as a young man. He would also, almost certainly get an opportunity to ride once again on his beloved red buses.

His Majesty King Richard under his beloved wife's guidance decided not to travel to London. He would instead watch the race on a 'Big Screen' television in the city's park together with the citizens of Artonia.

"That way," said Her Majesty "We will be able to share either the triumph or the disappointment of the day with our people. We will get through it together."

The King replied:

"It is my dearest absolutely the right thing to do. You are as ever my dear a wise old bird."

The Queen was not overjoyed at being likened to an "old bird" however wise it was. But she knew that her loving husband meant it as a compliment and she took it as that.

On the day of the team's departure a large crowd gathered by the palace gates to wave them off. As always in Artonia there was a bit of a party atmosphere with balloons, whistles and friendly heckling. The King decided to say a few words.

"We are delighted that after twenty four years Artonia is once again sending someone to compete in the Olympic Games." There were many cheers and one loud "Go Roly!".

"Her Majesty and I are particularly delighted and proud that it is our son Prince Roland who is representing our nation. Whatever the outcome of the race we know that he will do us all proud."

Someone in the crowd shouted out; "Three cheers for Prince Roly!" which everyone responded to with great gusto. Even the King and Queen joined in with the final: "And one for luck...Hip Hip Hooray!". And so after some royal 'good-lucks' and some hugs and kisses Prince Roly was ready to set off. Accompanied by Boris Morris his Official Coach and Erroneous Doodle his Official Team Doctor he climbed into the mini-bus. They set off on the long journey to London.

They were driven through several countries for many hours. Eventually they arrived in the middle of the afternoon at a famous train station in Paris the capital city of France. Here they boarded a special train which would take them under the English Channel all the way to London. As the train sped through the tunnel Roly leaned across and asked Boris:

"This train is great Boris, what is it called?"

"Eurostar Roly."

"That's nice of you to say so Boris," replied Roly. "But I haven't even raced yet, let alone won a medal or anything."

" No, no," said Boris "Not ...'you're a star'... Eu-ro-star."

"Ah! I see, I think. And why is it so dark outside, is it night time already?"

"No Roly, not night time, we are under the sea." explained Boris.

"Under the sea! But I can't see any fishies." said Roly peering out of the train window into the murk.

"We're not in the sea Roly we're under the sea. We're under the sea in a big tunnel. Do you see?"

"No I don't see. That's just the point. Can you see anything Doctor Erroneous?"

"Not a thing. We'll be better off when we're in London. "Then you'll see my beautiful red buses. They are the best way to travel."

Boris began to wonder whether his role as coach would also have to involve being minder and general take-carer of his two team mates.

In a few minutes the train pulled itself out of the tunnel and into the English countryside. In no time at all they were in London. Despite Doctor Erroneous's protests that a bus would be better, they clambered, together with all their luggage, into a big black London taxi. They sped off towards Windsor Castle. Both Boris and Roly were utterly amazed at the busy bustling streets that they travelled through. They had never seen such crowds of people, such numbers of cars and bikes and buses.

"My goodness Boris," said Prince Roly "It's like a thousand Artonias all stuck together in one giant jigsaw puzzle. How do the people know where they are or where they're going?"

Doctor Erroneous got excited. "They just jump on a bus with the right number, and it whisks them to where they want to go. It's simple."

He pointed out all of the landmarks that he recognised and that he remembered. He also told them about the routes and destinations of all the differently numbered red buses that they passed. The three of them were beaming with pleasure as the taxi pulled up to drop them off at the gates of Windsor Castle.

CHAPTER 17   ROYAL ENCOUNTERS

Two British Policemen met our three Artonian visitors as they left their taxi and approached the main entrance. One of the policemen spoke.
"Good evening gentlemen, and what might we do for you?"
Roly spoke up.
"Oh. Hello there. We are here to spend a few days with my cousin Elizabeth and, I'm in the Olympics you know. They are being held in London ."
"You don't say Sir. Well good luck to you, but I suggest in the meantime you turn around and see if you can't find somewhere nice to stay down in the town."
"But we're staying here. I am a Prince."
"Of course you are Sir, and I am a Maharajah."
"Are you really, wow, I've heard of those. Where's

your elephant?"

The policeman began to frown. "Now let's not be wasting police time shall we Sir. Joke over. Off you go now please."

His colleague began to move closer, with his hand resting on his truncheon. Boris stepped forward.

"Good evening officers, if I might help here. I have a letter from Her Majesty the Queen's under-under-secretary to Her Majesty's under-secretary's assistant secretary's assistant that explains it all. I think you will find everything in order." Boris handed over the letter.

The first officer read it through then spoke quietly to his colleague. He then turned about and spoke just as quietly into his radio. A few seconds later there was a muffled reply. He spoke again with the first officer. He then said,

"Very well Sir, I mean Your Majesty. Everything does seem to be in order. I do apologise for earlier, we cannot be too careful you know." The officer saluted.

"Oh that's perfectly all right," said Prince Roly returning the salute. "Scudamore is always very careful when opening our front door too. Good job officer, well done."

Roly saluted once more, and both the policemen stood to attention and saluted him back.

Boris tapped Doctor Erroneous gently on the shoulder to get his attention. He was distracted watching the stream of bright red buses that were going along the main road just down from the castle entrance.

They walked through the gate along the driveway towards the circular central castle. They were met by a very smartly dressed gentleman. He told them that his name was Wilson and he was a Royal Butler. It would be his pleasurable duty to look after them during their stay at Windsor. He helped them with their bags and led them towards the visitors' apartments.

There were a good many uniformed soldiers marching about the castle grounds and Roly was impressed.

"Look at these soldiers everywhere." he said.

"Yes indeed," said the good Doctor. "They are mostly here for lots of ceremonial parades and so forth. However, believe me, if anyone were ever to try and harm the Queen they would defend her to their very last breath."

"I say," queried Roly "Are there bad people after her?"

"She is a much loved lady" replied the Doctor, "but sadly not everywhere is as safe as Artonia Your Majesty."

"Why, the poor Queen. What a worry. We don't even have soldiers in Artonia."

"And for that Roly we should be very, very grateful." added Boris.

"I will and I am." replied Roly as a group of six soldiers marched by.

Roly stopped and saluted them. They stopped in perfect harmony, drew themselves to attention and saluted him back before turning and marching on. A shivery tingle went down the young Prince's back and suddenly he felt quite grown up.

They were shown to their rooms which were in a small tower in the centre of a large block. This was on the south side of the castle. They had a small bedroom each and there was a living room to share. This had the most splendid views across the lawns and parkland beyond the castle walls. Cutting through the lawns down a slope into the distance, went a very long and very straight pathway.

"Look at that Boris, a great place to practice my blading. I bet there are all sorts of paths leading off that one. I could cut back through in a big circle to the castle. What do you think?"

"I think it's a good idea Roly, but not tonight. We have had a long journey and we need some food, then some sleep."

Their royal butler Wilson soon returned with their meal which was presented on fine silver trays and the very best crockery. Having eaten well our Olympic team retired to their cosy bedrooms for a well deserved and peaceful night's sleep.

Wilson returned early the next morning, with their breakfast consisting of eggs, bacon, sausage, tomatoes, beans, fried potatoes, black pudding and toast. All this was washed down with freshly squeezed orange juice and a lovely perfumed tea called Earl Grey.

"Now I know," said Roly "Why they call it a 'Full English Breakfast', I'm full to bursting!"

Doctor Erroneous and Boris agreed, and they all decided it would be best to leave the training for an hour or so until their tummies had calmed down a bit.

An hour later they went out of the apartment and stood at the top of the long pathway. Boris had learned from Wilson that this was called The Long Walk. The doctor checked Roly's heartbeat and breathing and confirmed he was ready to start.

"Right," said Boris. "This first bit is The Long Walk Roly and it is all downhill."

"But surely I should use my roller-blades, that's what we're here for after all."

"Yes Roly you should use your blades but the path's called The Long Walk."

"Ah, I see." replied the puzzled Prince "Or at least I think I do."

"The path is called The Long Walk Roly, but you can roller-blade down it so don't worry. When you get to the bottom of the path turn left, and keep turning left until you come to Prince Albert's Walk and that will bring you back to us here."

"Will he mind?"

"Who?"

"Prince Albert."

"He's dead."

"Oh dear. I am sorry."

"He's been dead for over one hundred and fifty years Roly. The path is just named after him."
"Oh!" Roly said, still looking a tiny bit confused.
"Never mind Roly just get going. Okay? Three or four left turns and you should be back with us in about fifteen minutes. It's still a bit damp from some overnight rain. Mind the paths they could be slippery. Take it a bit easy on this first run please until you've got used to the route."

Off went Roly. Boris started his stopwatch while Doctor Erroneous made notes in his little black notebook.
"Medical notes doctor.?" asked Boris politely.
"No, no." replied the doctor. I am just trying to jot down a few bus routes in case we get time for a tour. I am sure you and His Majesty would love it."
"I am sure we would, but we only have a couple of days until the heat. We will have to see."
Meanwhile Roly had reached the bottom of The Long Walk. He had taken two left turns and was going through a wooded area. The path was uphill, but he was keeping up a good pace as it went around a large and very ancient oak tree. Roly took the bend at some speed with his head down. As he straightened up right in front of him stood four small dogs surrounding a little old lady. She was wearing a tweed skirt and jacket, dark sunglasses and a headscarf tied firmly under her chin.
The dogs began barking furiously as Roly applied

his brakes and tried to stop. He did so... just in time, but it caused him to skid on some wet leaves. He stumbled into a forward roll and landed with a painful squelchy bump on his bottom.
The four dogs pounced on him gruffling, snuffling and slobbering all over his face and hands. Their bark was indeed far worse than their bite. They continued to sniff and lick this strange young man.
"Stop it you lot," called Roly "I have already had my shower this morning."

With some considerable authority the lady spoke.
"Holly, Willow, Vulcan, Candy. Come away. Heel!"

All four dogs left poor Roly at once and went and stood in a very protective circle around the little old lady.

"Are you all right young man?" she asked.
Roly struggled up, brushed himself down and spoke:
"Yes thank you, I am fine, no damage done. I am sorry if I scared you."
"Oh no. Not at all." she replied.
"Are these your doggies?"
"Well yes, two of them are dorgis but the other two are corgis." she explained.
"Is a corgi not a doggie then?" asked Roly.
"No. Different breeds."
"Ah!" Roly was getting a little lost. "Do you live here

in Windsor?" he asked.

"Sometimes, yes." she said.

There was a moment's silence which was broken by one of the corgis barking impatiently. The lady continued.

"Well, if you are certain you are all right we shall be on our way. Good day to you."

"Good day." said Roly as he thought to himself 'I wonder if she works with Wilson up at the castle? Maybe she cooked us that lovely breakfast this morning'.

With that thought he set back off on his circuit and the little old lady continued on her walk with her four faithful pets...whatever they were.

When he arrived back at the top of The Long Walk the Doctor and Boris were both looking a little anxious.

"I know I said go carefully Roly, but you have been ages."

"I am sorry, but I slipped on some leaves and I was talking with this lovely old lady and her four..."

"Never mind chatting with old ladies. We've got a race to win. Please give him a quick check over Doctor, then we'll have another go."

Roly let the Doctor check him over. As he did so Roly was wondering what a corgis was if it was not a doggie.

Perhaps it was some sort of small bear?

CHAPTER 18   THE HEAT IS ON

The training went well after that with no other mishaps. Boris and the Doctor were delighted at Roly's progress and performance.

Soon it was the day of the heats. As they travelled to the Olympic Stadium by taxi (again much to the good Doctor's annoyance!), Boris talked tactics with the Prince.

"It's just the heats today Roly. You have to come first, second, third or fourth, okay?"

"Well make your mind up Boris I can't do all four."

"It doesn't matter which one you are just as long as you are one of them."

"Doesn't matter? But I thought that I came here to try and win?"

"You did, but it doesn't matter with this race. You can win the next one provided you come in the first four this time."

"So I can win even if I lose, as long as I don't lose. Is that it Boris? I'm getting a bit confused?"

"Listen Roly." Boris thought for a second. "Just go as fast as you can all right, and enjoy yourself."

Roly beamed, and Boris realised that tactic talks might not be a helpful idea with his young friend.

When they arrived at the Olympic Park they had to show special passes to get into the competitors' area. This was next to the stadium and you could already hear the crowd.

"Wowee. Listen to that. This place is enormous." said Roly getting quite excited.

"Now don't get too excited Your Majesty. We don't want your blood pressure going through the roof." advised Doctor Erroneous.

"I don't think it's got a roof Doctor listening to that noise." replied Roly.

Their event was up next. The three of them began making their way through a long dark tunnel. This was the entrance into the stadium itself. As they walked into the bright daylight of the arena the roar of the crowd, all eighty thousand of them, hit them like a thunderstorm.

"Oh golly gosh and diddly-dee," gasped Roly. "The whole world is here!"

Roly's eyes grew larger and larger and larger as he took in the scene all around him. He peered up into the towering stands at the thousands upon thousands of faces that all seemed to be staring straight back down at him.

As a race that was taking place neared its end the noise of the crowd grew even louder. It grew from a roar into an impossible wave of sound. It then crashed onto the beach splintering into a steady round of happy applause. Roly seemed to freeze. He was staring straight ahead across the arena.

"Are you all right Roly?" asked a very concerned Boris.

" I...I...I...I'mmm..." Roly began to wobble slightly. Doctor Erroneous stepped forward.

"Crowd shock! It's just like stage fright. Leave him to me."

Doctor Erroneous stood in front of the Prince bringing his two hands in front of Roly's eyes.

"Can you see my fingers Your Majesty?" he said in a loud and bossy voice.

"Fingies." muttered Roly.

"That's right, now look up what do you see."

"Fingies."

"No no, up a bit further where are the fingies, I mean, where are the fingers, pointing?

"Skysie wysie"

"That's good, and what colour is the sky?"

"A very pretty blue"

"So is it night time?"

"No it's day time silly."

"And what day is it?"

"It's my race day. It's the day of my heat"

"That's right, that's right, and what are you going to do in the race?"

"I'm going to win..." Roly's eyes blinked and he snapped back into focus "I am going to win my

race!"
The Doctor turned to Boris.
"All yours now Boris, he'll be fine."
Boris whispered the best of luck to his friend. He sent him off in the direction of the start where the other roller-bladers were lining up.
Roly joined the group who were busy tightening straps on their boots and doing some stretches. Roly said to them all in a big excited voice. "Hello you lot. This is fun isn't it?"
Two of the seven glanced over at him, but the others kept staring ahead. Roly thought they all looked a bit serious. Perhaps that was what he should do too.
He put on the most serious face he could, but the effort just made him want to burst out giggling. It was impossible for him to hold back and a great snort of laughter burst out. This made some of the others glare at him. Roly tried to control himself once more. It almost hurt. Just then the crowd went silent as a loud voice called the competitors under orders. "Take your marks, get set…" and then a pistol cracked and they were off.
Roly now did what he did best putting his head down and pushing off on his blades. The noise of the crowd faded from a roar to a whoosh as he went faster and faster. The racers were all in one group to begin with. After about three laps Roly and two others who were faster than the rest started pushing ahead.

Roly stayed with this pair tucked down just behind them both. He was really enjoying himself. The laps whizzed by and in no time at all a bell was rung. Roly knew it was time to speed up. It was the last lap.

The other two racers pushed ahead challenging each other. They powered into the back straight.

Roly gave a loud "whooo-hoo!" and kicked off as hard as he could. As they sped round the last bend into the final straight Roly drew level with the other two. He turned his head towards them winked and gave a quick wave with his left hand. He then pushed past them and swiftly crossed the finishing line in first place.

The crowd cheered and Roly waved to the crowd. The racer who had come second skated over to Roly and patted him on the back.

"Man," he said "You are something else."

"No I'm not," said Roly "I'm Roly." And he held out his hand. The other racer took it and shook it warmly, smiling.

"See you in the final man. I've got plenty more to give."

"Okay...man." said Roly "That should be great fun."

Boris and the Doctor came on to the track to congratulate Roly on his race. Then they led him away out of the stadium and safely back to Windsor Castle.

They were greeted in their apartments by their friendly butler Wilson. He provided them with a

delicious afternoon tea with scones and strawberry jam, and also announced that a message had been received from Roly's Father and Mother.
"Would you like me to read the message Sir?"
"Oh yes please Wilson. That would be lovely."
Wilson cleared his throat:
" Hmm hmm...A message from His Majesty King Richard Ricardo P. Nutt-Butter to his son Prince Roland Reginald P.Nutt Butter. Well done Roly we are all jolly proud of you. We watched your heat on the Palace television with Sir Quiggly and Scudamore. Goodness, but you did whizz. Good luck in the final Roly and remember winning isn't the important thing. Just take part and have fun. That is what it's all about. We will be in the Park with everyone else to watch you so good luck in the final. Give our best to Boris and Doctor Erroneous. We spotted them on the telly when they came on at the end of the race. Lots of love from Dad and Mum. We send you a big hug."
"Thank you Wilson that was lovely." said Roly.
"A pleasure Sir, and might I add that a few of us in the staff section watched your race on the television. It was most exhilarating. Our congratulations to you Sir."
"Thank you Wilson. That is very kind."
Wilson gave a polite bow and left the happy trio to their tea.

CHAPTER 19 FINALLY THE FINAL…JUST !

The next days were filled with a mixture of training and resting. Roly really enjoyed his practices in the Royal Park and was, as ever in continuing high spirits. In their time off they explored the castle's ancient rooms or played croquet on its beautifully kept lawns. They were kept well fed with the ever dutiful and cheerful Wilson looking after their every need.

On the evening before the final Erroneous approached Boris and Prince Roly with a proposal.

"As it is the day of the final race tomorrow, I would as team doctor advise that His Majesty rests from practice during the day. He will only need a a few

minutes warm up just before the race."
"Very good doctor. We will follow your advice." said Boris.
"Boring !" moaned Roly. "I'll just have to sit here all day. The race isn't until the evening."
"Ah ha!" replied Doctor Erroneous "I have thought of that too. As a distraction I suggest we go out for the day into London. With your permission and the use of the city's noble transport system I will give you both a guided tour. We will see all the famous landmarks of England's capital city. What do you say?"
"Rather!" exclaimed Prince Roly "Is that okay with you coach?"
Boris smiled and said; "What a splendid idea Doctor. We will have a super day I'm sure. It should stop Roly from getting too worked up about the final. It sounds like an excellent distraction."
"Wonderful." said the Doctor, "I have already drawn up a route. We start with a green line bus from Windsor to the city's centre, and then off we go on the wonderful red buses. I have it all worked out."
Boris spoke with Wilson who assured him that the Royal kitchens would be delighted to prepare them a suitable picnic for their day out. All was set for the next day. Prince Roly was very pleased.
"Wowee! A grand tour of London. A picnic lunch then off to the Olympic Stadium for my final. What could be better and simpler for our last full day in London."

'What indeed?' thought Boris to himself, keeping his fingers crossed that all went smoothly to plan.
After an early breakfast they set off from Windsor Castle. Doctor Erroneous carried a map and a timetable, Boris carried their picnic, and Roly carried a small backpack with his boots and race kit. They then took their first bus, a green one to start with, all the way to Victoria Station right in the heart of London.
"Right now, follow me boys. We will start with a number 24."
This followed the River Thames for some way then turned up towards Trafalgar Square.
"That," explained the doctor. "Is Nelson's Column."
"Why does he keep it here in the middle of London?" asked a puzzled Roly.
"It's called that because he's on top of it."
"That's a long way up, but I guess he's got a good view."
They crossed the road and caught a number 11 which headed up the Strand towards St Paul's Cathedral.
"Is it called St Paul's because he's on top of it, like Mr Nelson?" asked Roly.
"No no, that's just its name. It was built by Wren after the great fire."
"A little birdie built all that!" gasped the baffled Prince.
They then crossed another road to catch a number 8 heading back into Central London. After some

time the Doctor announced.

"Right, Oxford Circus. Time to get off this one."

"A circus, like my bedroom. Great. Where's the tent Doctor? Will there be clowns?"

"Sorry Your Majesty, no clowns, just another bus I'm afraid. We have to catch a number 12 to go down to the river and cross over at Westminster Bridge."

The Prince looked a little bit lost. Boris then cheered him up and quietly explained that London was a very old and important city and it remembered its famous citizens by naming roads and buildings after them.

They soon approached Westminster Bridge passing by the Houses of Parliament. Boris pointed to the tall clock tower.

"That Roly is Big Ben."

"Gosh it is big. Is there a Little Ben too?"

Boris smiled. "I am not too sure Roly, but if there isn't there surely should be."

When they had crossed the bridge they walked along a footpath next to the busy River Thames. They soon arrived at what looked like a giant bicycle wheel with glass rooms attached to it. It was called the London Eye.

"What is this?" asked a very excited Prince Roly.

"A surprise Your Majesty. This is the London Eye, a giant ferris wheel. We're booked to go on it in ten minutes. A good place for the picnic I thought."

"Brilliant idea Doctor." said Boris " You'll be able to

see all over London from up there Roly. You will even be able to see Windsor Castle and The Olympic Stadium!"

"Ooooh fantabulous! And we get to eat the picnic?"
"And we get to eat the picnic."replied Boris.

The trip on the 'Eye' was as good as possible on a bright clear day. They saw most of the places they had been to in the morning and all the places they were to visit during the afternoon. This included Buckingham Palace the London home of Her Majesty The Queen

The rest of their bus tour went smoothly. They ended up right outside of Buckingham Palace to watch the soldiers marching. Our weary trio then decided to go into the beautiful park next door to the palace. They sat by a lake to feed some ducks and geese with the left overs of their picnic.

It had been a hot August day and they decided to have a short rest lying on the lush grass. They had plenty of time before having to think about getting to the stadium.

Six eyes, that's three pairs, all tightly shut. They all became lost in dreams.

Doctor Erroneous dreamed that he was driving a number 9 bus all the way up The Mall to visit the Queen. Boris dreamed of his lovely family. Doris, Horace, Norris and Floris (Morris Minor) all chatting excitedly to him around the breakfast table. Roly dreamed he was racing around the Olympic track. He was chasing the little old lady with the headscarf and dark glasses. She was on a pair of sparkling roller boots and way ahead of him. Behind poor Roly with snapping teeth and angry barks were the lady's four dogs. They were getting closer and closer.

A steady deep ringing sound began to make its way into in each pair of ears.

Roly thought it was the bell for the last lap and tried to speed up.
Doctor Erroneous thought it was the bus's bell asking him to let someone off at the next stop.
Boris, counting the deep bongs in his waking head thought it was the old grandfather clock at home.
One, two, three, four, five…SIX!
"SIX !" shouted Boris sitting bolt upright.
"No, not six ..Number nine." called the doctor still completely sparko.
"There are four !" said Roly, "but they can't catch me."
"No, no you two…wake up. It's six o'clock. Your race Roly. It starts in one hour."
"Oh, that's good then. I've got time for another snooze" murmured Roly curling himself up into a snuggly ball like a hedgehog.
"No you don't Roly. You have to get going. Come on now. Wakey-wakey."
Doctor Erroneous slowly came to. He stood up and stretched himself awake. He then helped Boris to

wake up Roly who at last came to.

"So my race starts in just one hour from now. Oh goody."

"Less than an hour Roly. So quickly now, pop your kit on and we'll go and find a taxi."

In just a few minutes they were again outside Buckingham Palace trying to flag down a taxi. Every one they saw seemed to be busy and the minutes were ticking furiously away. Eventually after what seemed like hours, but was really just ten minutes, an empty taxi spotted them and picked them up.

The taxi driver spoke to them as they clambered into the back of his cab.

"Where to Governor?."

"The Olympic Stadium please," asked Boris. "Our friend here is in a race at 7.00 o'clock. Please go as fast as you can."

"I'll do my best Governor, but the roads are choc-a-block tonight. It's Friday and everyone's either getting out of town for the weekend or going to the stadium."

"Well just do your best... please?" asked Boris.

"Will do Gov'. Hold on to your hats gents!"

With that the taxi whizzed off back towards the Houses of Parliament then down by the river. They made great headway with the driver seeming to know every sort of traffic dodge and shortcut. But, just as they thought it was all going well, they turned onto the main road at Whitechapel. This was to take them down through the East End of London to the stadium. The road however was packed with vehicles all stood still. The traffic was making virtually no progress at all. The clock was turning ever faster towards seven o'clock.

The driver did his very best, but no amount of bobbing and weaving was helping.

"I hate to say this, but I don't think you're going to make it gents." said the driver. "By my watch you've got less than fifteen minutes and I just don't think well get there in that time. I am so sorry."

Roly looked glumly at the floor of the cab. The Doctor looked out at the traffic piled up in front of them. Boris began to think.

"The stadium's further down this road, is that right driver?"

"Yes Governor, another couple of miles then it's off to your left. You can't miss it."

"Roly, get your boots on. You can dodge this traffic, and that'll be your warm up. Come on, don't just sit there! You've got a race in a few minutes, and friends back at home waiting to watch you."

Roly , then said with a great smile,

"Right! Well done Boris. I knew you'd sort it out."

In just a minute Roly had his boots on. He quickly climbed out of the taxi. The driver directed him.

"Just keep going straight down this road until you see the Stadium on your left. Good luck mate."

"Go on Roly. We'll see you at the finish. Enjoy yourself." said Boris patting his friend warmly on the shoulder. Roly smiled at Boris.

He gave a loud 'Yahoo!' and then took off, speeding quickly towards the Olympic Stadium.

"Yeee Haa!" he yelled as he began to slither and snake between all the cars, buses and vans that were stuck still like sculptures cluttering the road.

Roly was on his way.

CHAPTER 20 THE BIG FINISH

Meanwhile many hundreds of miles away in the Royal Park in Artonia the excitement was building. The King and Queen were sat with crowds of citizens happily awaiting Prince Roly's race. It was just minutes before the start. The competitors for the final were coming out onto the track.

"I must say my dearest," began King Richard "I do not think I've been so excited for ages, not since I last beat you at snooker."

Queen Flotilla knew that King Richard had never beaten her at snooker. She allowed his fantasy to live on in his cheerfully muddled head. She too was very excited about Prince Roly's race and in no way wanted to spoil the occasion.

There was some muttering now amongst the crowd as everyone focussed upon the giant television screen. Someone in the crowd called out: "Where's His Majesty? Where's Prince Roly?"

Their Majesties too studied the screen and sure

enough in the line of competitors there was one space in the middle. There was in this space no sign of the Prince. The other competitors were lining up and preparing themselves for the race.

"Where' is our Roly?" said Queen Flotilla quite anxiously.

"He'll turn up, he's bound to." replied the King, who was now beginning to get butterflies in his tummy. The worried crowd in the Royal Park grew quiet.

Back in the approach road to the Olympic Stadium Prince Roly was pushing himself harder and harder. He could see the competitors entrance ahead with a large clock above it. That read exactly 7 o'clock. He heard the crowd inside become hushed and a moment later the sound of the starter's gun. The race had begun.

Roly showed the security guards at the entrance his competitor's badge as he whizzed by them into the tunnel that went through to the race track.

In the Royal Park the mood had switched from really, really excited to really, really glum. King Richard had reached out for Queen Flotilla's hand and was giving it a re-assuring and comforting squeeze. All of a sudden the crowd gave a united and enormous collective gasp.

"It's Prince Roly !" they exclaimed in unison.

The cameras on the screen had turned briefly from the speeding racers now into their second lap. They zoomed in on the image of the Royal Artonian. They showed him entering the arena from the competitors' tunnel, crossing the start line and beginning his race. The Olympic Stadium erupted in cheers. This was echoed just as loudly in the Royal Park where glum had gone and joyous excitement had returned.

"There's our little chap." shouted King Richard.

"He never was too good at telling the time." said Queen Flotilla before forgetting herself completely and bellowing like thunder "Come on Ro!y! Catch them up!"

Prince Roly was really motoring by now and although he had started over a lap behind was indeed catching up at a great rate. Within a few laps he had not only made up the lap but was overtaking the tail-enders. On he whizzed, cheered by the spectators in London and his friends and countrymen back in Artonia.

In no time at all a bell was sounding. It was the start of the last lap.

Still just in front of Prince Roly were three racers. They were being led by the man he had beaten in the heat. The three leaders kicked off for the finish, and Roly chased them down.

As the final lap continued Roly began to overtake his rivals. First he was third, then he was second and as they turned into the last bend he was closing in on the leader.

"Come on Roly!" screamed Queen Flotilla who in

her excitement had stood on her chair which she was now riding like a horse in the Derby.

"Go Roly...go Roly...go Roly!" screamed the rest of the Artonian supporters. The crowd at the stadium too were on their feet. The noise was unbelievable.

Closer and closer drew Prince Roly as he and his rival approached the finish line at enormous speed. There were a thousand camera flashes that exploded in a spray of white light as the two crossed over the line side by side.

Roly and his rival drew up quickly and without a moment's hesitation embraced each other in celebration. It had been an amazing race.

"Man you were unbelievable, you came out of nowhere." said the racer.

"Well, not nowhere actually." said Roly. "I came from somewhere called Whitechapel. Jolly lucky to make it at all to be honest."

The crowd grew silent as the display board signalled that it had been a photo finish. The judges were examining the images to see which roller-blader had won.

Queen Flotilla had jumped off her chair and was now hugging King Richard tightly as they awaited the result. Boris and Erroneous had arrived in the arena just as the race was ending. They too were now standing on the trackside watching and waiting.

There was a sudden crackle on the loudspeakers. The announcer spoke, as the display board put up the results of the race.

"Ladies and gentlemen, in an Olympic first the judges have declared that there was no distance at all between the two competitors at the finishing line. They have therefore declared a dead heat. The gold medal winners are therefore from Cuba, Juan Carlos De Martinez and from Artonia, Prince Roland Reginald P. Nutt-Butter.

"Man," said Juan Carlos, "that is sure once fancy name, Your Majesty."

"Oh please, all my friends call me Roly. You have quite a fancy name yourself Juan Carlos." At this the young Prince stretched out his hand which Juan Carlos warmly took and shook.

Boris and Doctor Erroneous ran quickly over to join in the celebrations along with the other competitors.

Back in Artonia the crowd had gone completely crazy. Music had begun, party poppers were popping and everyone was hugging everyone else.

A few minutes later the medal ceremony was held. When Roly and Juan Carlos received their medals everyone in the stadium applauded warmly. In the Royal Park everyone grew very proud and emotional. Tears of joy streamed down the faces of both the King and Queen as the Artonian and Cuban flags were raised side by side and their anthems played.

In the stadium Boris and Doctor Erroneous stood next to each other. Each was thinking to themselves privately that this was one of the proudest days of their lives.

Prince Roly just smiled the biggest smile you could ever imagine. He could not wait to get home and show his gold medal to his Mum and Dad.

CHAPTER 21   SIR QUIGGLY COMEAR'S NEWS

When the Olympians returned the next day to Artonia large and excited crowds came out to cheer and say a very loud and proud
"Well Done Prince Roly!"
Roly's Mum and Dad were of course delighted with him. They had prepared an enormous celebration. Tea with cakes, scones, butterscotch popcorn and sausage rolls. All of which were amongst the Prince's favourites.

A great deal of fuss was quite rightly made by everybody. Miss Gloria 'Scoop' Da Loop the editor and journalist of ANT's came along. She took a great many photographs of Prince Roly, Boris, Doctor Erroneous and naturally the King and Queen. They all stood next to one another and admired the Olympic Gold Medal. She also took a photograph of the Prince holding his very first pair of Roller Boots. This was the very pair that she had given him on the occasion of his sixth birthday. Gloria was very proud that it was she who had introduced Prince Roly to the sport. She was just delighted that he had now a dozen years later become an 'Olympic Champion'.

The next day things calmed down considerably. Life went as far back to normal as was possible at the Royal Palace. The sun rose, clocks ticked, the sun set. Days, weeks and then months went happily by. All was good, all was calm.

One spring morning a few months later Sir Quiggly Comear made an appointment to visit the Royal Quarters and speak with Their Majesties.

The King spoke as Sir Quiggly entered their palace apartments.

"Ah ha, Sir Quiggly my dear fellow. What news, what news?"

"Your Majesty will bear with me I hope, but I have two pieces of news for you today."

"Two, Sir Quiggly?" said a surprised Queen Flotilla. "Why, you spoil us. We normally get one or two pieces of news a month and here we have two in one day. Shall we cope with the excitement I wonder?"

"No news is often good news Your Majesty." replied Sir Quiggly wisely.

"So, is it bad news Sir Quiggly?" asked King Richard.

"Well that Your Majesty would depend on your point of view." said Sir Quiggly.

"My point of view?" asked the King

" Yes Your Majesty. We all see things differently. I cannot see things through your eyes, only you can."

King Richard starting looking around the room to see what it was perhaps that he could see that Sir Quiggly could not.

"Ah ha! Is it my new slippers that are behind the sofa?" asked the King.

Sir Quiggly was a tad confused and looked towards Queen Flotilla hoping for rescue.

"I think Sir Quiggly that it might be best if you just give us the news now, before things spiral out of control."

"Thank you Your Majesty. The first news is that I have received a letter from the King of Rasberria. He is undertaking a grand European tour next month and he wonders if he and his family might spend a few days with Your Majesties here in Artonia."

"Do we know the King of Rasberria Ricardillo?"

"Oh yes my sweet. His name's Bungo and he was at that awful school when I was. He was a nice chap. He used to let me share his tuck on Fridays. Of course he wasn't a king then, just a prince as I was. It would be great fun to see him again and catch up."

"Very well Sir Quiggly that all seems jolly." said Queen Flotilla. "Would you kindly let King Bungo know that we would be delighted to have him and his family stay with us next month."

"Certainly Your Majesty."

"Okay Sir Quiggly," said King Richard "What's the next bit of news?"

"Ah well Your Majesties, that is a little more personal. Might I sit down?"

"Of course dear chap. Do take a seat."

Sir Quiggly sat in a large red armchair and suddenly looked quite small and frail. He put his hands together between his knees, and glanced across at the King and Queen. He took a deep breath and continued.

"As you may know Your Majesties this summer I shall be celebrating my eightieth birthday."

"Bravo Sir Quiggly. What a what a wonderful party we shall have." interrupted King Richard.

"Quite so Your Majesty, thank you. But I do feel now that it would be a very good idea to retire from my post. I believe it is time now to make way for a younger man."

"Retire? Impossible! What on earth would we do without you?" said the King.

"Now, now, Richard. We must not be selfish. Sir Quiggly has worked here at the palace since he was a young man. He deserves to stop and put his feet up."

"Of course you are right my dear. Sir Quiggly my dear fellow, of course you may retire. But I will miss you. You've been looking after me ever since... well, ever since I can remember."

"I know Sir, and it has been an honour and a

privilege. But now I just wish to tend to my garden, and enjoy my happy memories. I will still be living here in the palace grounds I won't be far away. As regards my replacement, I would strongly recommend my secretary Scudamore. He has been helping me more and more lately. He really is a most excellent fellow."

The King and Queen smiled across to each other and then both stepped forward to shake Sir Quiggly warmly by the hand.

"For now," said Sir Quiggly "If you will excuse me it is business as usual. I shall not leave my post until my birthday. In the meanwhile, there is a royal visit to prepare."

Sir Quiggly bowed politely and left the Royal apartments.

"Not sure I like change that much my dear." said King Richard.

"We shall manage my darling. Time does not stand still. I am certain that Scudamore will make a first class Chief Advisor."

"Fancy Sir Quiggly wanting to retire. Having all that time to himself. I think I might get a little bored."

"Bored Ricardillo? Really?"

"Well yes. I mean, what would we do if we had all that free time?"

"Why dearest we would be able to do lots of things. Have some adventures."

"Adventures Flotsie? Do tell."

Queen Flotilla thought a second smiled and continued.

"Well we could do all the things that we have talked about doing, but have never had the time to do because of our royal duties."
"Do remind me my sweet. My head is as empty as a thirsty bucket."
"Well, let me see if I can think of anything. Oh yes I can."
Her Majesty took a very large breath then continued.
"We have talked about how we like to have a try at: abseiling, bungee jumping, canoeing, deepsea diving, elephant welfare, ferreting, golfing, horse riding, igloo building, jousting, kangaroo spotting, llama farming, mountaineering, nature rambling, orienteering, para gliding, quad biking, rock climbing, shark fishing, tobogganing, U.F.O. spotting, volcano climbing, white-water rafting, xylophone, yachting and zoo- keeping."

Her Majesty gasped and took a second deep breath.

"My goodness Flotsie that is a list and a half, and they all sound such fun."
"Yes Richard. Perhaps being retired is not quite such a boring idea."
"No indeed Flotsie. Perhaps it is not."

With those thoughts very firmly planted deep within their royal heads Their Majesties began to think about their future years together and the many new exciting adventures they might have.

Sir Quiggly on the other hand returned to his office. With the help of his secretary, the very able Scudamore, he began to make the more practical plans for the future visit of King Bungo of Rasberria and his family.

CHAPTER 22   ROYAL VISITS

Everything was put in place to make the royal visit a great success. King Bungo T. Kettle, his wife Queen Ocean and their daughter Princess Tallulah were to enjoy one day of public events. This would begin with a grand parade to be followed by a visit to an Artonian Blue Dairy.   In the evening there would be an open air concert in the palace grounds. The second day would be a private day for the two families.

The parade went very well, with large numbers of the good people of Artonia turning out to wave, cheer and generally join in the fun. King Bungo and Queen Ocean then went to visit one of the nation's most celebrated cheese makers. Here the process of producing the famed Artonian Blue Cheese was demonstrated, explained and of course tasted.

"I say Ricky this really is most awfully good." said King Bungo

"Thanks Bungo. We are jolly proud of our cheese."
"How come it tastes of spearmint?" asked Queen Ocean.
"Well," replied King Richard "It is a bit of a trade secret, but basically on top of all the scrummy blue grass we feed the cows, they also have a couple of pieces of bubble gum each day."
"Bubble gum by Jove? Are you pulling our legs Ricky?"
"No, no they love it. They chew away for hours and blow the most amazing bubbles. Come outside and have a look."
The four royals scuttled outside into the farmyard where the cows were queueing to be milked.
"I say, there goes one now!" said an excited King Bungo.

Sure enough one of the cows close to where they were standing stopped chewing for a moment and started to blow. A bubble of blue tinged gum began to grow from the animals tightly pursed lips. Larger and larger it grew until after a minute the bubble was just a little bit bigger than the contented creature's head. There was then a loud and significant "pop!" The bubble burst and spread itself all over the animal's face. The cow blinked twice in surprise. Its huge tongue then slid out of its mouth and, rather like a circular windscreen wiper, licked its face clean. It took the gum back into its mouth to start chewing once more.

"My goodness," exclaimed Queen Ocean "I have never seen anything like that before, just like the teenagers back home," and she began to laugh. The others joined in and the four royals carried on with their most enjoyable day.

Back at the palace Prince Roly had been asked by his parents to entertain Princess Tallulah. She had told her parents in very clear terms that she was not going to look round a "blooming smelly old cheese factory!"

Roly who had never met a princess before was trying to be polite. He was trying to find something to do that she would enjoy. He was having little luck so far.

"Would you care to look around the palace gardens?" he asked.

"I am sure the trees and plants won't take offence if I don't bother." she replied.

Roly tried again.

"How about a game of monopoly or scrabble?"

"They are called board games because that's what they do…bore you."

Another dead end thought Roly. He had another idea.

"We could go and visit the cathedral, it's full of statues and tombs and stuff."

"So you want to go and look at dead people. Excuse me, but I'll be excused."

Roly was getting frustrated and so asked.

"Well give me a clue Tallulah...what do you like to do?" he asked in desperation.

"Anything exciting... I thought you'd be fun being an Olympic champion and everything. Not look at flowers and dead people."

"Well sorry, but I thought princesses liked that sort of stuff. I've read the story of the princess and the pea you know."

"Think again then. I am not that sort of princess. I like adventure!"

"Wow!" said Roly. "Me too. What do you like?"

"Well I like Judo for a start. That's exciting."

"Judo? I've never tried that. Is it easy?"

"No. But once you're good at it, it's great fun. Shall I show you."

"Rather!" replied Roly.

With that Princess Tallulah moved towards him and quickly grabbed his jacket. She stepped in close, span around and flipped him over her shoulder in one fluid movement. Roly lay flat on the floor looking up at the Princess who was still firmly gripping his jacket. He beamed an enormous smile. Tallulah smiled back.

"That was fantastic." said the Prince

"Thanks." said Tallulah

"Show me again."

Tallulah showed him again, and again, and again! A little shaken Roly asked if she might teach him how to do it too.

"Only if you show me how to speed skate. I'm not very good at that, but I'd love to learn."
There then followed an hour or two of skating and judo lessons that wore them both out.
"That's been great fun Roly. Shame we can't carry on this evening. We've got that stupid concert to go to."
"Oh it won't be that bad. Mum's arranged for some acrobats, a juggler and a fire eater too. They will liven things up a bit."
Roly thought for a minute.
"We could liven it up a bit too. Give everyone a bit of a surprise."
"Oh do tell, what's your idea?" asked Tallulah
"Well…are you afraid of heights?"
"Of course not." she replied.
"Then I have an idea. We could add a little something to the entertainment. What do you say Princess Tallulah?"
"I say that's brilliant Prince Roly. Tell me more."
With that the two young royals set off to prepare their surprise.

King Richard and Queen Flotilla arrived back at the palace with King Bungo and Queen Ocean. They wanted to get themselves ready for the evening's entertainment.
They were met by Scudamore the secretary to, and soon to be successor of, Sir Quiggly Comear Chief Advisor to the Royal Family.

"Your Majesties, King Bungo, Queen Ocean, welcome to the palace. Everything is ready for the evening's concert if you would like to follow me."

"Scudamore," asked Queen Flotilla "where are our Roly and the Princess Tallulah?"

"They wished to be excused for a while Your Majesty. They are enjoying playing a game of chess and will join you at the concert when they have finished."

"Chess!" exclaimed King Bungo "Tallulah, playing chess. By Jove Ricky your lad has had a good influence on our girl. Never heard of her playing chess. Ever!"

"Well I must be honest Bungo. I didn't know our Roly knew how to play the game."

"I am just glad they are getting on. Our Tallulah can be a little headstrong." said Queen Ocean

"Well let's leave them to their game shall we. The concert can't start until we get there, and there should be quite a crowd. Lead on please Scudamore." said Queen Flotilla.

"Of course Your Majesty." replied Scudamore smiling gently to himself. The Prince and Princess had told him about their planned surprise, and he was in on the secret.

CHAPTER 23   WHAT AN ENTRANCE

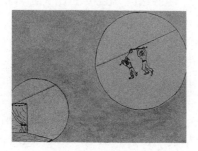

The King and Queen and their Rasberrian guests walked through the palace gardens and down to the meadow.This is where the stage had been set up for the concert to take place. Across the field in front of the stage a large crowd of excited citizens had gathered to enjoy the concert. Everyone had brought a picnic to make it a real night out.

As the royal party arrived everyone stood up and there was a round of warm applause. The four friends took their seats in front of the centre of the stage.

"I say Scudamore" asked King Richard. "What's that cable doing strung down from the palace to the stage?"

"Oh!" said Scudamore "That is something do with the lighting. It will get dark in half an hour or so."

"Ah yes of course. Would you like a cake

Scudamore?"

"No thank you Your Majesty. I have already had something to eat."

With that there was a drum roll from the Royal Elastic Band. As ever they were in charge of the music for the evening. At last the entertainment began. All of the acts were local people from the city and surrounding villages of Artonia. What they lacked sometimes in skill and talent they made up for with much enthusiasm and humour. So when the unicyclist wobbled and the tumblers tumbled perhaps a little bit too often they were still heartily clapped and cheered. Everyone had come to enjoy themselves, so that is what they did. Songs were sung by the school children, and they performed some energetic country dancing.

"Where could our children have got to?" asked Queen Ocean "They are missing all the fun."

"Oh I am sure they'll be dropping by any time soon Your Majesty." said Scudamore.

At that moment there was another drum roll, the stage lights were dimmed and a spotlight shone back towards the palace. In the mixture of bright light and the gathering darkness of the evening the crowds could not make out whatever it was the spotlights were trying to illuminate.

Then, slowly, a shape began to appear in the distance. It was just below the roof of the tower at the back of the palace. The shape sparkled and grew clearer. It appeared to be some sort of strange creature with four legs dangling beneath it. Voices in the crowd called out:

"Is it some sort of giant birdie?"

"I reckon it's a dragon."

"No, no, I think it looks like some sort of aeroplane with legs!"

There was much laughter and excitement as the object picked up in speed and grew larger. It became clear it was sliding down the large cable that was attached to the stage. Everyone's eyes adjusted to the light and the object came into view.

Whizzing down the wire on a trapeze bar came two figures hanging on tightly and whooping with joy.

"Yaaaaahoooo!" screamed Prince Roly.

"Zippy-dippy-doooo!" bellowed Princess Tallulah.

"That's our baby!" Queen Ocean gasped.

"Crickey!" said King Bungo "That is our Tallulah. Go! Tallulah Go!"

"Chess my Aunt Nelly! Go Roly! That's my boy!" called Queen Flotilla loudly.

The two trapeze artists flew over the crowd's heads and fluttered down towards the stage where they slowed down and stopped right in its centre. Their feet were just a step above the stage. They unclipped their safety harnesses and jumped down. Turning around they were greeted by thunderous applause from everyone including their delighted parents. They took a bow, and left the platform to join their Mums and Dads.

"Chess indeed Roly." said King Richard.

"Sorry Dad, we just thought we'd liven things up a little."
"Tallulah, what do you have to say for yourself?"
"Can we do it again please?"
"Tallulah!" they all chorused and then there was much laughter and some well-earned hugs.

The Royal Elastic Band started playing again and everybody danced. The concert finished with an amazing fire-eater and some spectacular fireworks. Everyone began to make their way back towards their respective homes. The Royal Group trudged happily back towards the palace wishing each other a very good night's sleep. They all agreed how much they were looking forward to a quiet day together the next day.

Roly and Tallulah were the last to get back to the palace.
They had collected up the trapeze and safety harnesses.

Inside the palace hallway Roly said goodnight to Tallulah.
She smiled at the him and said,
"That was the best fun I have ever had Roly. Really, really great. Thank you Roly and goodnight."

With that she leant forward and gave him a very quick kiss on the cheek. She smiled again and then ran up stairs to the rooms that her family were staying in.

Scudamore came into the hallway from the kitchen and saw Prince Roly standing staring up the stairway frozen like a statue.
"Are you all right Your Majesty?" he asked.
Roly did not move or blink. Scudamore coughed a polite cough and spoke again.
"Your Majesty. Prince Roly. Are you all right. Is everything okay Sir?"
Roly woke from his dream.
"Ahhh, I was just er, that is, she um, well, err. Right oh Scudamore. Nightie, nightie."
"Pyjama, pyjama Your Majesty." replied a bewildered Scudamore.

Roly ran up the stairs two at a time and went to bed.

Scudamore watched as the Prince disappeared in a blur. He thought to himself that it must be all the excitement. It must have gone to the young man's head. He locked the palace doors and took himself wearily to his rooms.

CHAPTER 24   CLIMB EVERY MOUNTAIN

The next morning King Richard and Queen Flotilla were amazed to find that Prince Roly was up, washed and dressed by seven o'clock. Normally he would have to be dragged reluctantly from his bed much later in the day.
"Good morning Mama. Good morning Papa." he said.
"Mama?" queried the Queen
"Papa?" echoed the King "Are you all right Roly? You aren't feeling ill or anything?"
"No, no. Far from it. I feel absolutely tickety-boo. I thought this morning that I might mountain biking if that's all right with you. I suppose I don't mind letting Princess Tallulah drag along with me. If you thought I should. Being sort of polite and everything."
"That would be very good of you Roly," said his mother "You two certainly seemed to be getting on very well yesterday."
"No we didn't."

"But you did."
"Well I mean she is okay I suppose, but it's not like we're best friends or what have you. She certainly isn't my girlfriend."
"Nobody said she was." said his father.
"Exactly! Well there you are then, I mean I don't even want a girlfriend anyway. I am just going to whizz one of the bikes over to Boris. The breaks need adjusting. Right! Better dash."
Roly left his parents' room, thundered down the stairs and out of the palace front door. Queen Flotilla spoke first.
"Oh dear Ricardillo I think our little boy' been smitten."
"Really? Who's smit him?"
"Smitten Ricardillo. I mean he may be taken with Tallulah."
"Taken? Where to?"
"Oh Richard do wake up. I think our Roly may have fallen for Tallulah. And before you say it, I do not mean he has fallen over."
"Ah, I see…I think?"
"He likes her Richard. He may want her as a girlfriend."
"But I heard him say quite definitely he did not want a girlfriend."
"I know. He said it about ten times."
"Well that proves it Flotsie. He doesn't want a girlfriend."
"I am afraid Ricardillo it proves exactly the

opposite. He never usually twitters on like that. Nor is he up at the crack of dawn washed, dressed and ready to go out. Our little boy may be falling in love."

"But I don't understand Flotsie. Do you mean that when a chap says he doesn't want something, that it really means that he does want it?"

"Yes Richard. That is because he is a man and women understand men." said Flotilla.

"So, do you understand me my dearest?" asked the King.

"Of course I do Ricardillo. I understand you better than you do yourself."

"Well that's good, because I don't have a clue what I'm on about half the time." said the King.

"I know Richard, and that's why I fell in love with you all those years ago."

"Oh Flotsie, you are lovely. I only hope Roly falls in love with someone as lovely as you."

Just along the corridor in the visitors rooms Princess Tallulah was having a very similar conversation with her parents.

"Oh and by the way I don't mind hanging around with Prince what's his name today, if I really have to. I mean he is all right and everything I suppose. Not that I want him as a boyfriend or anything."

"Well that is fine my dear." said Queen Ocean "Because nobody asked you to."

"Thank goodness, that's what I say. I don't even

want a boyfriend anyway. I'll go and change into my jeans and trainers. Just in case he wants me to do anything. Just so I can be polite. Okay?"

Princess Tallulah went back to her room to get ready.

"I say old girl" said King Bungo "What's up with Tallulah rambling on about boyfriends and such?"

"It means dear Bungo that our little girl may have taken a shine to Prince Roly."

"Taken a shine? Does he need dusting?" asked Bungo.

"No Bungo. Taken a shine, you know. She likes him." replied Queen Ocean.

King Bungo continued the conversation.

"But she just said she didn't want a boyfriend."

"Which means she does."

"But she said the opposite ?"

"That proves it."

"Proves it? How?"

"She is a woman. We do that sort of thing."

"Do you indeed?"

"Of course."

"So, do you my love say one thing meaning the opposite?"

"Never darling."

"Which I suppose means pretty much all the time. Not sure I quite understand."

"That dear Bungo is just the point. Now come along, we are to join Richard and Flotilla for breakfast."

said Queen Ocean finally.

Down in the palace dining room the four royals shared a good breakfast and compared notes on the blossoming friendship between their two youngsters. Both Bungo and Richard were very strongly warned by their respective wives not to 'interfere' and not to say anything!

It was just then that the two youngsters came into the dining room.
"Morning folks. Princess Tallulah and I would like to go mountain biking up in the hills. Is that okay with everyone?" asked Roly.
King Richard was about to speak when Queen Flotilla tapped him firmly on the shin with her right foot.
"Ouch!" went the King.
"No problem at all Roly." replied Flotilla.
"Prince Roly has made some sandwiches so we won't need any lunch if that's okay?" asked Princess Tallulah.
King Bungo went to speak when his shin too received a warning tap from Queen Ocean.
"Oof!" went the second King
"You two have a good time." said Queen Ocean.
"We will see you this afternoon." added Queen Flotilla.
Roly and Tallulah walked awkwardly out of the dining room. They disappeared out of the palace

grounds on their bikes.

"Well" said Queen Flotilla "I think that went very well."

"I agree" said Queen Ocean.

Kings Richard and Bungo sat rubbing their respective shins. They wondered what they had done wrong and what on earth all the fuss was about.

CHAPTER 25   LOOK OVER
YOUR SHOULDER

Roly and Tallulah swiftly pedalled through the city streets and were soon on a narrow country lane. They headed up into the hills that surrounded the outskirts of the city. After a few minutes they both stopped.
"This is where we leave the road Tallulah," said Roly "It's a bit bumpy and it's all pretty much uphill. Are you okay with that?"
"Of course I am Roly," said Tallulah, "I think you have gathered that I am not a wimp."
"Yes, dead right I have. We'll take it easy though. It is quite a climb, but the views from the top are a-ma-zing!"
"Brilliant!"
They set off at a steady pace following an old goat track They rode up along a ridge towards the top of the hill.
It was a glorious sunny afternoon but a light breeze

helped to keep them cool as they made the climb. They stopped twice for a breather and a drink of water. After one final big push they reached the summit. They got off their bikes and took off their helmets and backpacks. They sat on a large rock to eat their sandwiches.

"The view is just as a-ma-zing as you said Roly."

"It is pretty cool isn't it. You can see right across the city to the hills on the other side of Artonia."

"Is that the palace just there behind the cathedral."

"Yes that's it, home. What's Rasberria like Tallulah?"

"Well it is about the same size as Artonia, but we have more woodland and maybe a few less farms. There are some mountains to our south side where we can ski in the winter."

"Oh wow! I've never been skiing. We don't ever get enough snow here."

There was a long pause as they both munched their way through the Artonian Blue Cheese and pickle sandwiches Roly had made for them.

"Tallulah?" said Roly

"Yes Roly."

"I'm sorry you have to go tomorrow. You're great fun to be with."

"I'm sorry too Roly. I have lots of friends in Rasberria, but I've never met anyone as crazy as you."

"Crazy? Do you think so? Really?"

"Absolutely bonkers. Just like me."

"You are a bit bonkers Tallulah. I like that."
"Do you Roly? Do you like that I'm a bit bonkers?"
"Absolutely. You could be the Queen of Bonkersville."
"And you could be the King of Crazy."
They both laughed and then it fell quiet. Roly broke the silence once again.
"When my Mum met my Dad she says she knew straight away that he was the one for her." said Roly.
"How did she know Roly?" asked Tallulah.
""She says it was a funny feeling she got in her tummy."
Tallulah paused for a few seconds and then said.
"Roly."
"Yes."
"I think I might have that feeling in my tummy."
"Oh, it's probably just the cheese and pickle sandwiches."
"Don't be crazy!"
"Can't help it. I'm the King of Crazy" laughed Roly.
"Completely bonkers." replied Tallulah smiling too.
"The King and Queen of Completely Bonkers Crazyville."
"Sounds good to me." said Tallulah

Once more they fell silent but held each other's gaze for a few moments before looking away a little embarrassed.
A shadow fell as a cloud bubbled up in front of the

sun. A gentle and distant rumble of low thunder broke the silence.

"We had better get going soon Tallulah. It looks as if we might get a storm."

"Okay Roly." said Tallulah with a big sigh.

"Come on Tallulah, cheer up." Roly stood up and put out his hand to help her up from the rock. As she did so she stepped in close to him and gave him a second quick kiss on the cheek."

"Gosh Tallulah, why did you do that again?" he asked feeling very confused.

"Because it makes my tummy feel better." said Tallulah and she smiled warmly. Roly beamed back at her. His face grew a lovely rosy red.

They stood in a kind of half-trance for a few moments until there was an enormous flash of lightning and a crack of thunder. It echoed dangerously around the hills. They both stepped back.

"We really had better get going."

"I'm with you Roly."

With backpacks on and helmets secured they set off down the ridge along the goat-path towards the road. The rain began to spit great globs of water.

"If we stay on this path and don't go on the road it's a much quicker route back." said Roly.

"I'll follow you. You lead Roly."

They cut across the hillside heading down towards the edge of the city. The ground grew quite a bit bumpier and it was criss-crossed with shallow streams. The rain was really beginning to fall now. Both of them were finding it hard to see ahead. The water ran down their faces.

"Are you okay?" shouted Roly looking back over his shoulder.
"I'm fine. Keep going." called Tallulah.

Roly pressed on, and kept looking back to make sure Tallulah was all right. It was during one of these glances over his shoulder that he did not see a boulder looming up before him. Princess Tallulah did see it and yelled.
"Look out Roly!" But, it was too late!

His front wheel hit the boulder square on bursting the tyre and buckling the wheel rim. It caused the bicycle to flip up and throw the young heir of Artonia some several feet into the air. He continued forward in that direction for several more metres. He landed, with a very hefty bump, bottom first in a rocky stream.
"Yeeeow!" yelped Roly not knowing whether to hold his sore backside or grab his right ankle. This had received a nasty twist and was already beginning to throb painfully.
Tallulah jumped off her bike and ran to his side.
"Roly! Are you okay?"
"Yeah…a bit better than my bike I think. I've given my ankle a bit of a twist when I crash landed."

"Can you stand up?"

"Not sure. I'll try."

He put his arm around Tallulah's shoulder. With her arm around his waist for support he managed to stand up.

"What about walking?" she asked.

"I might be able to hop a bit. Can you help me back to the boulder. It may have been my enemy, but it can be my friend now and let me sit down."

With her help Roly hopped back to the boulder and sat down. His ankle was very sore, but he didn't think any bones were broken. The rain was still pouring and flashes of lightning and thunder continued to rumble and grumble. Tallulah then took charge.

"Right Roly. You sit here. It looks as if the storm will soon roll away. I can see the road ahead so I'll go on back to the palace to get help. I'm afraid I can't carry you by myself."

"Hold on Tallulah. I thought the hero was supposed to rescue the princess?"

"Not in this story Roly. Now sit tight and don't try to move."

With that Tallulah gave Roly the third polite kiss on his very soggy cheek. She then jumped on her bike and sped away down the hill.

Prince Roly watched as she disappeared. Something warm and lovely lit him up inside. He almost forgot that he was actually in quite a lot of pain, sat on a rock, at the bottom of hill in the pouring rain.

Princess Tallulah raced back to the palace to raise the alarm. Within minutes Scudamore and Boris were on their way to fetch Prince Roly back from his damp and rocky resting place. When they arrived you would have thought that Prince Roly was already safely snuggled up on the sofa back home with a hot chocolate and a toasted tea cake. He looked so happy and contented.

"Hi you two." he called as they approached. "Any chance of a piggy back?"

CHAPTER 26   A STEADY PAIR OF HANDS

The next morning saw everything calm at the Palace. King Bungo and Queen Ocean had asked if they might extend their stay by a few days. Their excuse was that it would help Princess Tallulah recover from the shock of the accident. The real reason was to allow the young couple a little longer to get to know each other. To see how their friendship might develop.

Doctor Erroneous Doodle popped in to check on Roly's progress. He had bandaged up his sprained ankle the evening before. He brought a wheelchair for the Prince to use and prescribed a painkiller for his poorly foot.

He suggested a big cushion for the other part of the Prince's anatomy that had been injured and was indeed very tender!

"How did you take your tumble Your Majesty?" asked the doctor as he examined the ankle.

"We were whizzing down this hill when Princess Tallulah saw this huge rock but I didn't."

"Why did she see it but you didn't?" asked Erroneous..

"I was looking back at Tallulah to make sure she was all right.!"

"But she was, wasn't she?" queried the doctor.

"Yes she was fine, but then Kaboom! I took off like a blooming rocket."

"Might I offer Your Majesty a small word of advice?"

"Fire ahead Doctor Doodle. You have always looked after me so well. I shall welcome your advice."

"That is my point I suppose. If you are going to look after somebody it is important that first of all you look after yourself. Otherwise you may end up not being able to look after them at all." said Erroneous. Prince Roly took time to take in what Doctor Erroneous had said. He then replied.

"Thank you doctor, message understood. I'm no good to anyone if I come a cropper."

"Exactly Your Majesty. Now I had better carry on. More customers to see. Ding-dong move down the bus and so forth. Remember no hopping on that foot. Use the wheelchair for a day or two and take it easy." instructed the doctor.

"Will do doctor. Cheerio, and thanks again."

Miss Gloria 'Scoop' Da Loop had popped into the palace to try and get some information for the story about the Prince's accident. Roly was delighted to see his old friend, and Princess Tallulah joined them to tell her side of the story.

Roly kept trying to say what a hero Tallulah had been. But she really wanted her part in the story played down.

At the end of the interview Gloria asked if she might take a photograph of the Prince and Princess to go with the story. They went into the courtyard with Tallulah pushing Roly in his wheelchair.

"If you stand behind His Majesty please Princess Tallulah. And Prince Roly if you could just sit up a little that should be fine?" asked Gloria. She peered through the eyepiece of her camera. After some seconds she looked up.

"You two look far too happy for a post-accident photo. Could I ask you to look a bit more serious, or glum or maybe just shocked."

Roly and Tallulah tried their best to look seriously sad. The effort was too much and they burst out laughing

"I am sorry Miss Da Loop," said Roly "Have we spoiled the picture?"

"I guess not Your Majesty. The people will be pleased to see you looking so happy. They will be worried about you after your accident. This will put their minds at rest."

"Oh good. Thanks then Miss Da Loop. See you again soon."

Tallulah pushed Roly out of the courtyard and into

the palace gardens.

Gloria could not help but wonder about those happy smiles. Were they all about surviving the accident, or were they more about a blossoming friendship?
However Miss Gloria 'Scoop' Da Loop prided herself that ANTs was not one of those gossipy sort of papers. The article she would write would not mention anything other than the facts of the accident and the happy outcome. She did however allow herself to smile at the prospect of a royal romance. With that lovely thought she packed up her camera and roller-booted back to her office.

Scudamore and Boris were talking in the palace kitchens. Boris had come to see if his friend Prince Roly was okay.
"Thank you so much for helping last night Boris." said Scudamore.
"No problem Scudamore. It's not the first time I've had to help Roly out." said Boris.
"You have known His Majesty a long time haven't you Boris" replied Scudamore.
"Oh yes. We met on his first day at school and we've been good friends ever since."
Scudamore thought for a moment and then continued.
"You have heard that Sir Quiggly is retiring soon Boris and I am to be made the Chief Advisor."

"Yes I have heard. You'll be brilliant I am sure." said Boris.

"Thank you. I will need an assistant to work with me. I need someone to take over the job I've done with Sir Quiggly all these years. Might you be interested in such a position ?"

"Me?" said a surprised Boris "But I know nothing about running a country."

"But you do know a great deal about Prince Roly. You showed last year at the Olympics you're a good organiser. This is very much a hands on job. Looking after the Royal Family on a day to day basis. Making sure they don't get into too many scrapes. What do you think ?"

There was quite a pause then Boris spoke.

"I think I need a little while to think about it if that's okay. I would have to discuss it with Mum and Dad. Mum works here at the palace already and she might find it a bit funny with me working here too. Of course I think I'd like to ask Roly what he thinks. I would not want it to spoil our friendship. It means too much to me."

Scudamore was impressed by Boris's thoughtfulness and that convinced him even more that he would be perfect for the job.

King Richard and Queen Flotilla were resting in the shade of an apple tree down in the orchard. They had just been playing a ferocious game of tennis with their Royal Guests. Queen Ocean had paired up with Flotilla to play against Bungo and King Richard.

In the card game called poker a pair of Kings always beats a pair of Queens. In this game the two Queens had whopped the two Kings winning six games to love.
A complete whitewash!

"I say Flotsie old Bungo is not too good at tennis. He missed all the important shots." moaned the King.
Flotilla as usual was much too kind to point out that her husband had missed twice as many important shots as Bungo. Neither did she add that Richard had as usual run around a bit like a headless chicken. He had chased every ball and missed most of them.

"Never mind dearest, you did your best." comforted the Queen.

She continued
"It seems that Roly is on the mend now, so we can relax and think about the future."
"The future? What, space travel and what- not?" asked the King.
"No dear. I was thinking about Sir Quiggly's retirement."
"Ah yes, that's next month. I have asked Scudamore

to organise a surprise party for him. It should be great fun." said the King.

"I am sure it will be my sweet. Then perhaps we can think of planning for our retirement." said the Queen.

"But we can't really Flotsie. We've got a job for life."

"Nonsense Ricardillo, that is such an old fashioned idea. Lots of Kings and Queens retire these days. They let their children take over the throne."

"That is our problem then. We only have one child, and it's Roly." said the King.

The Queen spoke again.

"Our son is now a young man Richard. He is no longer a child. A perfect time to hand over. Let him take the reins of reigning!"

"But Flotsie, much as I love the boy dearly, he is a bit scatty. How on earth would he manage?"

"Richard, you have managed beautifully for over thirty years and you are as daft as a daffodil. Are you not my sweet?"

"Of course I am Flotsie. I put the nut into P. Nutt-Butter. But I have got you, Sir Quiggly and Scudamore to help keep my feet on the ground."

"And Roly will have good people. We won't be far away either. I believe he may also have a very good wife in Tallulah."

"Are they married then, did I miss that?" asked the King.

"No dear they have just met, but I have a strong

feeling she will be his bride."
"Really! How can you tell?"
"I have the same sort of feeling as I had the day I met you my darling. I wasn't wrong then was I?"
"No Flotsie. The best day of my life when you knocked on my door."
"As it was for me Ricardillo. Our son, Prince Roly has a big heart, just like his father. That is why the people will love him just as they love you."
"That sounds wonderful Flotsie." said the King. "You do know I love you more than anything don't you Flotsie."
"Of course I do Ricardillo, and I love you too."

They started to stroll through the orchard. They talked about the adventures they would have when they had retired. Flotilla assured her husband that his son would make a very fine King especially if he has Tallulah's steady pair of hands to guide him.

At that very moment they heard an enormous screech followed by loud 'whoops!' and 'yahoos.'
They stepped beyond the trees just in time to witness Prince Roly thundering down the pathway on his wheelchair. Princess Tallulah was stood up on the back holding on tightly yelling for all she was worth and urging him on.

"The steady pair of hands of Princess Tallulah?"

asked the King.

"Well," said the Queen "She hasn't fallen off yet has she?"

They smiled at each other then started to laugh until tears ran down their cheeks. They turned and watched the future rulers of Artonia as they rattled to a halt by the farm buildings. As they watched them they wondered what marvellous adventures would await them. They knew that whatever happened it would be accompanied by a lot of love and laughter.

Printed in Great Britain
by Amazon